Property Taxation: The Need for Reform

Property Taxation: The Need for Reform

Karl E. Case

Ballinger Publishing Company • Cambridge, Massachusetts
A Subsidiary of J.B. Lippincott Company

This book is printed on recycled paper.

International Standard Book Number: 0-88410-485-0

Library of Congress Catalog Card Number: 78-9850

Printed in the United States of America

Library of Congress Cataloging in Publication Data

Case, Karl E.
  Property taxation.

  Bibliography: p. 119
  1. Property tax—United States. I. Title.
HJ4120.C35   336.2'2'0973
ISBN 0-88410-485-0

To My Parents

Contents

List of Tables

List of Figures

Preface

For criticisms and helpful suggestions I am deeply grateful to Richard A. Musgrave and John F. Kain. A number of my former students helped with the tedious job of collecting and coding data. Among them were Cristoph Berendes, Susan G. Cole, Thomas Gennis, Barbara Jaffe, and Ngozi Okonjo. While Susan and Kristen Case had primary responsibility for keeping me productive and reasonably cheerful throughout, a substantial number of others contributed. Worthy of special recognition were Jayne Doughty, Jayne Niesloss, Marlene Carter, Marshall Goldman, Susan Levin, Yvonne Quinlan, and the students at North House. For substantive comments as well as good cheer I am indebted to Ed Lazear and Dutch Leonard. The manuscript was typed in several stages by Karen MacKensie, Cathy Durovich, and David McClamrock. Financial support was provided by the Ford Foundation grant number 680-0040 to Harvard University and Wellesley College.

KEC

Property Taxation:
The Need
for Reform

✳ *Chapter 1*

Introduction

Public sector revenues in the United States come almost entirely from five major types of taxes: (1) personal income taxes, (2) payroll taxes, (3) corporate income taxes, (4) sales taxes (both general and selective), and (5) property taxes. While property taxes have declined as a percentage of total tax revenues from 51.4 percent in 1902 to 15.0 percent in 1975, they remain the primary source of local government revenues. In 1975, 81.6 percent of local tax revenues came from property tax collections[1].

Since the property tax is locally administered, some consider it the only tax over which taxpayer voters exercise direct control. As a consequence, it is not surprising that it is the subject of much public discussion and debate. Such debates are rekindled annually when localities announce their tax rates for the coming year. They generally focus on the size of the rate increase, the general burden of the tax, and the need for property tax "relief."

What is surprising is the seeming lack of knowledge and concern about the way in which property tax burdens are distributed among taxpayers within jurisdictions. Taxpayers seem to view their tax bills as if they were prepared in a black box programmed to assign the burden in an appropriate and fair way. Yet precisely in those jurisdictions where tax rates have risen most dramatically have large differences in "effective rates" of taxation among individual taxpayers arisen.[a]

---

[a]"The effective rate" paid by an individual taxpayer is the annual tax bill divided by the market value of the property being taxed.

1

Boston represents a dramatic example. Announcement of the tax rate by the mayor each year is greeted with considerable fanfare. The story is carried with banner headlines on the day of the announcement, and general discussion continues for weeks. In the same city, a routine examination of public documents reveals effective tax rates on residential property that differ by a factor of 10. That is, there are individual property owners who pay up to ten times as much as others with nearly identical properties. Such inequalities have evoked little public outcry.

One might speculate that this lack of public debate results from the fact that assessments have not changed through time. Annual revenue increases are more often than not generated through rate increases rather than assessment increases. Thus, attention becomes focused on the changing rate rather than the level and pattern of assessments. One might also argue that since most properties are only assessed at a fraction of their market values and since increases in market value are only infrequently reflected in assessment increases, many homeowners think they are getting a "good deal."

Whatever the reason, the issue of burden distribution seems to emerge only during the infrequent and usually painful process of revaluation. During revaluation, tax burden is reassigned, tax bills change, and voters are aroused. Some find bills decreased while others are faced with dramatic increases. Where administration of the tax has been poor and where differences in effective tax rates have grown large, the process of moving toward accurate and uniform assessment may be blocked by the potential of a taxpayers' revolt.

Such is the case currently in Massachusetts where the city of Boston is under court order to reassess all property at 100 percent of true value[2]. Implementation of the order will result in a massive shift of tax burden among residential neighborhoods and among individual property owners within neighborhoods. In addition, the overall portion of the tax borne by residential property will rise dramatically vis-à-vis commercial and industrial property.

This book will attempt to answer a series of questions regarding variation in effective property tax rates within taxing jurisdictions. How much variation is there within jurisdictions? Are the enormous inequities observed in Boston typical or atypical of those in other U.S. cities, urban and rural? Why do such inequities arise? Are they consciously created by tax administrators and politicians, or are they the result of administrative errors and poor assessment procedures? Finally, what are the implications of the present state of affairs and what can be done about it?

The book is organized into four substantive chapters. Chapter 2 empirically examines the extent of variation in rates. Chapters 3 and 4 attempt to sort out the causes of observed variation. Chapter 5 deals with some implications on intrajurisdictional rate variation; specifically, it explores the extent to which tax differentials are capitalized into land values.

Previous work on property tax rate variation has focused on differences *between* taxing jurisdictions. Such differentials arise out of inequalities on both the capacity and need sides of the fiscal equation. This is, districts with substantial amounts of commercial and industrial base may tax residential property at a lower rate, and districts that face high costs of public service provision or that choose high levels of service provision must tax at a higher rate.

While the problem of interjurisdictional differentials in property taxation has generated a substantial volume of economic literature, the issue of intrajurisdictional differentials has only recently been addressed[3]. Henry Aaron suggests that this gap exists because "for economists, especially, the subject of tax administration has carried none of the allure of 'analysis' or 'policy', but only the drabness of bureaucratic affairs"[4]. This book will argue, on the contrary, that variation in rates within jurisdictions is a problem of considerable analytical interest as well as public policy importance.

Before proceeding, it is important to define the problem facing fiscal administrators. The property tax differs from the other major sources of public sector revenues in a number of important ways. Most significant is the fact that its base is fundamentally different from other major revenue bases.

First, the base of the property tax is a stock rather than a flow. Flow variables such as income and sales generally represent the value of some set of specific recordable transactions that occur in a given time period. As such, they pose few serious conceptual difficulties for fiscal administrators. If accurate records of interpersonal and interinstitutional transactions are maintained, measurement of sales and of most income components is not difficult.

The most significant exception is the problem of computing asset gains. Economic income includes on the uses side, consumption plus any net increase in wealth. As such, accurate measurement of true income would involve complete valuation of all real assets at the end of each time period. The problem has been circumvented by relying on sources side transactions data to obtain a close second-best approximation. Capital gains are included in the base only when realized. It has been shown that full inclusion of nominal gains as realized is a fairly good second-best solution since the undertaxation of asset holders resulting from the deferral of taxes on accrued gains to the time of realization is closely balanced by the overtaxation resulting from taxation of nominal rather than real gains[5].

While the problem of asset valuation has become of secondary importance to those concerned with the design of income tax law, it remains absolutely central for those concerned with property taxation. The base itself is a stock and as such must be valued each period. Transactions data alone, while of some help, are insufficient for two reasons. First, individual pieces of real property generally pass through the market only infrequently. The average holding period for an owner-occupied home or a piece of business property is significantly longer than that for shares of common stock or bonds. In the Boston area only about 3 to 5 percent of assessed properties are sold during any one year.[b]

Second, real property is extremely heterogeneous, making the imputation of the value of one piece of property from the sales prices of similar properties a nontrivial task. This is not so for most commonly held liquid assets such as stocks and bonds. Portfolio evaluation is a relatively simple task since shares of G.M. stock are homogeneous and a market price is posted daily.

[b]The number of transactions was obtained from *The Real Estate Transfer Directory*, published by Auto Data Systems, Framingham, Massachusetts, for 1971 and 1973. The number of assessed properties was obtained from records on file at the Massachusetts Division of Corporations and Taxation, Bureau of Local Assessment. For 1973, selected results are shown below:

Percent of Assessed Properties Sold During 1973

City	Percent
Arlington	4.8
Cambridge	4.7
Newton	5.1
Waltham	2.9
Wellesley	4.6

Chapter 2

The Extent of Intrajurisdictional
Variations in Effective Rates

EARLIER STUDIES

There is an extensive empirical literature documenting the extent of intrajurisdictional variation in effective property tax rates. Most studies focus on assessment ratios and effective tax rates on single family nonfarm houses. This is true for several reasons. First, in terms of number of properties assessed this represents by far the largest single property classification. As such, there are large amounts of readily available data and fairly well-established assessing procedures within jurisdictions.

Second, many jurisdictions classify properties and consciously assess at different rates across classifications. For example, most large cities negotiate property tax rates with large commercial or industrial concerns. Most assessors will readily admit to such practices even when they are not permitted *de jure*, as in Massachusetts. However, assessors without exception claim to strive for accuracy and uniformity within the category of single family nonfarm housing. Within the past two years, the author has worked in twenty-six local assessing offices obtaining data on single family housing units. A careful review of procedures in those jurisdictions provided no evidence of a conscious bias in assessing within the classification of single family nonfarm housing. This is not to argue that systematic biases do not exist. On the contrary, the remainder of this book will demonstrate the existence of rather dramatic biases. However, the argument is that the bulk of the bias results from poor procedures and time lags rather than conscious efforts to assess properties at different rates.

The most comprehensive source of data on assessment rates is the census of governments conducted every five years by the Census Bureau. In 1972, enumerators gathered information on just under a quarter of a million property sales that took place during a six-month period of 1971[1]. Of these sales, 112,000 survived a careful screening process and were used to compute assessment-sales ratios for the 2,000 jurisdictions in the study. Jurisdictions were chosen to reflect a cross section of types and sizes within each state.

As a measure of dispersion, the Census Bureau opted for relative deviation around the median ratio. The coefficient of intra-area dispersion was calculated as

$$D = \sum_{i=1}^{N} \frac{|x_i - \tilde{x}|}{N\tilde{x}} \qquad (2\text{-}1)$$

where x_i = Ratio of assessed value to sales price
for property i
$\tilde{x}$ = Median assessment-sales ratio for the
jurisdiction
N = Number of transactions in the sample

The results of the census study are astounding. Nationwide the median coefficient for single family houses is 20.2. This means that roughly half the taxing jurisdictions in the sample err by an *average* of 20 percent on all properties assessed. The implication is that a very large number of properties are either over or underassessed by more than 20 percent. In Massachusetts, the median value of single family homes in the census sample was $27,000[2]. The median effective tax rate for sampled jurisdictions in Massachusetts was 3.8. The value of a 20 percent overassessment on a $27,000 home with an effective tax rate of 3.8 percent is roughly $3,400.[a]

Table 2-1 presents a tabulation of dispersion coefficients by city size. It indicates two things. First, as one might expect, the distribution of coefficients is flatter for areas of less than 50,000 than for areas of more than 50,000. That is, while a larger percentage of smaller towns have very low coefficients, a larger percentage of smaller towns have coefficients over 40 and over 50. This reflects the tremendous differences in assessing procedures that can be found outside of metropolitan areas.

[a]This assumes a discount rate of 6 percent and an average life of forty years.

Table 2-1. Distribution of Coefficients of Intra-Area Dispersion for Single Family (nonfarm) Houses for Selected Local Areas: 1961, 1966, and 1971

(Cumulative percentages of total number of ratios)

Coefficients of Intra-Area Dispersion (percent)	All Selected Areas			By Population					
				Area Population 50,000 or More			Area Population Less Than 50,000		
	1961	1966	1971	1961	1966	1971	1961	1966	1971
Less than 10.0	2.9	7.6	6.7	1.8	4.4	3.7	3.6	9.8	8.8
Less than 15.0	13.7	28.2	24.6	11.9	30.2	22.7	14.7	26.8	26.0
Less than 20.0	29.9	53.4	48.9	32.8	60.8	52.1	28.3	48.4	46.6
Less than 25.0	47.6	69.1	67.0	57.5	76.7	72.3	41.9	64.0	63.2
Less than 30.0	61.9	80.4	79.1	75.1	88.0	84.4	54.3	75.4	75.3
Less than 40.0	80.6	90.2	90.9	92.9	94.7	94.4	73.5	87.3	88.4
Less than 50.0	89.4	95.7	96.1	98.2	98.2	98.3	84.2	94.1	94.6
50.0 or more	10.6	4.3	3.9	1.8	1.8	1.7	15.8	5.9	5.4

Source: U.S. Department of Commerce, Bureau of the Census, *Census of Governments 1972*, vol. 2, no. 2, Table J, p. 14.

Second, while there is evidence of improvement in uniformity between 1961 and 1966, there is no such evidence for 1966-1971. In fact, if anything, the data reveal a reversal of the earlier trend. In part this is due to increased uncertainty and higher levels of economic activity during the later period, which undoubtedly led to changing patterns of property values. This is particularly true of 1971 when the last sample of sales was drawn.

Finally, what emerges powerfully from these data is that property assessment nationwide is quite inaccurate. Recall that this discussion has focused only on single family nonfarm houses. Table 2-1 indicates than in 1971, 5.4 percent of sampled jurisdictions with population greater than 50,000 and 1.7 percent of those with population less than 50,000 had *average* assessing errors of *more than 50 percent*. There were a total of 90 such jurisdictions in the sample of 2,000 areas. If assessments had been done with a random number generator drawing from a uniform distribution over the real line bounded by the highest and lowest observed values, the coefficient of dispersion would be approximately .75.

In addition to the published Census data, there have been a number of empirical papers that have examined the extent and pattern of deviation in assessment ratios within jurisdictions. Perhaps the earliest was a study of Frederick Bird that analyzed assessment ratio data from the *1957 Census of Governments* and concluded that within a substantial number of jurisdictions the situation "is one of an almost incredibly wide range of administrative performance"[3]. Bird found that while 20 percent of taxing jurisdictions displayed what he called "good" procedures, another 20 percent of the areas displayed results that were "unbelievably poor."

The best known and most frequently cited study is Oldman and Aaron's study of Boston[4]. Oldman and Aaron obtained information on nearly 14,000 property transfers that occurred in 1962 from the Metropolitan Mortgage Bureau in Boston. Grouping the data by location, property type, and price, the study examined both the extent of variation and pattern of variation in assessment rates. As a measure of dispersion within each classification, Oldman and Aaron use the standard deviation of the assessment-sales ratio.[b] Table 2-2

[b]Standard deviation of a random variable, x, is defined as $\sqrt{v}$ where:

$$v = \sum_{i=1}^{N} \frac{(x_i - \bar{x})^2}{N-1}$$

where $\bar{x}$ is the mean of the sample.

Table 2-2. Assessment-Sales Ratios for Residential Properties in Boston, 1961-1962

	Boston	*East Boston*	*Brighton*	*Charlestown*	*Dorchester*	*Hyde Park*	*Roxbury*	*West Roxbury*	*South Boston*
Mean Assessment Sales Ratio	.442	.281	.329	.393	.351	.314	.541	.311	.369
Standard Deviation	.211	.096	.095	.169	.133	.190	.237	.090	.176
Number of Observations	104	27	85	13	339	218	37	499	31

Source: Oldman and Aaron, *op. cit.*, p. 40.

presents their results for single family homes. In their words, the study reveals "plenty" of inequality and "many kinds" of inequality in assessment. In Boston, a mean of .44 and a standard deviation of .21 implies that roughly one-third of the properties sampled have assessment-sales ratios greater than .63 or less than .23.[c] It is important to note that Oldman and Aaron do not attempt to explain their observations. They state: "the study has revealed systematic inconsistencies in property tax assessment . . . . Explanations for this pattern are obscure"[5]. A more detailed breakdown of their results will appear later in this chapter for comparison with 1973 data.

The most exhaustive study of interjurisdictional variation in assessment ratios was accomplished in 1969 by David E. Black[6]. Black obtained data on approximately 18,000 individual transactions in the city of Boston that occurred during the years 1950 and 1960 from the Metropolitan Mortgage Bureau. The data were an exhaustive sample of transactions chosen from roughly 155 census tracts.

Black's data simply confirm the picture painted by the Oldman and Aaron study and demonstrate that things got worse in Boston between 1950 and 1960. Basic tabulations of his results are presented and compared to Oldman and Aaron's results in Table 2-3.

In each of the three types of property classification, the standard deviation as a percentage of the mean assessment-sales ratio rose

[c]This assumes a roughly normal distribution around the mean ratio.

Table 2-3.   1950 and 1960 Assessment to Market Value Ratios, Boston

	Black 1950	Black 1960	Oldman and Aaron 1962
Single Family			
Mean Ratio	.56	.38	.34
Standard Deviation	.22	.18	.15
Standard Deviation/Mean	.39	.47	.47
Number of Observations	2352	2133	1353
Two Family			
Mean Ratio	.60	..43	.41
Standard Deviation	.18	.16	.19
Standard Deviation/Mean	.30	.37	.46
Number of Observations	1976	2102	780
Three Family			
Mean Ratio	.73	.53	.52
Standard Deviation	.21	.20	.27
Standard Deviation/Mean	.29	.38	.52
Number of Observations	2426	2150	746

Source: David E. Black, *op. cit.*, p. 63; Oldman and Aaron, *op. cit.*, p. 40.

considerably between 1950 to 1960 and again between 1960 and 1962. Since the data are not disaggregated by section of the city, they seem to indicate even more inequality than do the data employed by Oldman and Aaron, which are presented in Table 2-2. However, when Oldman and Aaron aggregate across sites, their results are consistent with Black's.

PERFORMANCE IN THE 1970S

The current study updates the earlier work with data on sales that took place during the 1970s. In order to maintain comparability with the Black and Oldman/Aaron studies, data were obtained on just over 650 recorded transfers that took place within the city of Boston proper. In addition, the study examines data on over 2,400 sales of properties located in the Boston suburban ring and more than 3,000 sales in nonmetropolitan regions of ten states.

The Data

Information on properties that were transferred in the Boston area was obtained from Auto Data Systems (ADS), a private corporation in Framingham, Massachusetts. Annually ADS publishes for each Massachusetts county a volume called the *Real Estate Transfer*

Directory, which lists all deed transfers recorded in the county for the year. Transactions are listed alphabetically by street address and are subclassified by taxing jurisdiction and sometimes subdivision. For each sale, the directory lists buyer, seller, amount of sale, amount of mortgage, holder of mortgage, and type of property.

ADS was not the primary source of data. Their information is obtained from the registry of deeds in each individual jurisdiction. Although sales price is not recorded directly on each deed, excise stamps are affixed that reflect the full transaction's price. Relative to other states, where tax avoidance is often widespread, the accuracy of this method of obtaining sales information seems to be extraordinarily accurate in Massachusetts. ADS verifies approximately 15 percent of its observations and claims an error rate of less than 1 percent. More than twenty sales were personally verified, and no errors were found.

Assessed values for Boston area properties were obtained from one of two sources. The Bureau of Local Assessment of the Massachusetts Department of Corporations and Taxation is required to maintain copies of assessment records for all cities and towns. Failure to report by many jurisdictions has resulted in outdated and incomplete records. Although some assessments were obtained centrally, most were obtained from the files of individual local assessing offices. Property assessments are public records and are generally filed by street address.

Sales price data on the nonmetropolitan properties were more difficult to obtain. While excise stamps were affixed to deed transfers in all areas, there was evidence of frequent tax avoidance through underreporting of sales values. Most county clerks seemed to have no inclination to scrutinize transfers more carefully. As a result, other sources of data were required, and several were utilized short of household interviews. In a minority of sites, aggressive assessors themselves had obtained information on sales values. However, the primary source was the files of local real estate agents. In each town there was at least one agent who attempted to keep a complete file on all sales within the jurisdiction. Where such data were obtained, efforts were made to cross-check at least 15 percent of the observations with either a second source (agent or assessor) or through personal contact with the owner. Assessments were again obtained directly from assessors.

Results

Tabulations for the city of Boston based on 1973 sales reveal that the dispersion of assessment-sales ratios and thus the dispersion of effective tax rates has grown since the time of the Oldman and

Table 2-4.   Assessment-Sales Ratios for the City of Boston 1960–1964 and 1973; Residential Property

	1960–1964[a]	1973
Boston Subdivison		
Mean	.49	.28
Standard Deviation	.23	.14
Standard Deviation/Mean	.46	.50
Number of Observations	171	50
Dorchester		
Mean	.42	.34
Standard Deviation	.19	.33
Standard Deviation/Mean	.45	.98
Number of Observations	1043	266
Roxbury		
Mean	.65	.37
Standard Deviation	.25	.32
Standard Deviation/Mean	.38	.85
Number of Observations	137	111
South Boston		
Mean	.47	.19
Standard Deviation	.23	.09
Standard Deviation/Mean	.49	.46
Number of Observations	121	93
East Boston		
Mean	.44	.24
Standard Deviation	.15	.11
Standard Deviation/Mean	.33	.46
Number of Observations	99	106
West Roxbury		
Mean	.33	.20
Standard Deviation	.09	.10
Standard Deviation/Mean	.26	.47
Number of Observations	685	39

[a]See Oldman and Aaron, *op. cit.*, 1940.

Aaron study. Table 2-4 presents results for six subdivisions of the city of Boston. In each division, the mean ratio has declined substantially as assessments lag behind property value increases. The distribution of subdivision means has not changed a great deal; the lowest ratio is about 50 percent of the highest. The mean ratio has fallen most rapidly in South Boston and most slowly in Dorchester. Roxbury remains the most heavily assessed while West Roxbury remains at the bottom, now tied with South Boston.

Most significantly, the dispersion of rates around subdivision

Table 2-5. Assessment-Sales Ratio Distributions for Sixteen Jurisdictions in the Boston Suburban Ring[a]

	Bedford	Belmont	Concord	Lincoln	Reading	Stoneham	Wakefield	Wellesley	Weston	Waltham	Saugus	Melrose	Arlington	Cambridge	Chelsea	Somerville
Mean Ratio	.47	.76	.79	.57	.82	.33	.31	.68	.60	.78	.86	.91	.84	.26	.29	.25
Standard Deviation	.06	.10	.11	.12	.07	.07	.05	.09	.14	.21	.18	.14	.30	.18	.12	.07
Number of Transactions	151	168	163	22	230	123	152	315	133	214	168	171	185	208	42	22
Standard Deviation/Mean	.13	.13	.14	.21	.09	.21	.16	.13	.23	.27	.20	.15	.36	.69	.41	.28

[a] All sales took place in 1971 with the exception of those in Cambridge, Chelsea, and Somerville, which took place in 1973.

Table 2-6. Assessment-Sales Ratio Distributions for Ten Nonmetropolitan Jurisdictions[a]

	Paris, Tn.	Hamburg, Ar.	Jesup, Ga.	Raton, N.M.	Williamston, N.C.	Uniontown, Pa.	Cambridge, Md.	Uvalde, Tx.	Cuero, Tx.	Hanford, Ca.
Mean Assessment Sales Ratio	.80	.66	.36	.26	.66	.60	.41	.43	.14	.86
Standard Deviation	.73	.15	.09	.09	.13	.24	.20	.31	.06	.15
Number of Observations	172	310	.62	.81	155	212	522	99	202	1089
Standard Deviation as Fraction of Mean	.91	.23	.25	.35	.20	.40	.49	.72	.43	.17

[a]Sales for 1972-1975 were adjusted to 1975 limits using a price deflator estimated from an examination of properties that had resold in subsequent years.

means has grown in five of the six sampled areas.[d] In Dorchester and Roxbury, the standard deviation as a fraction of the mean ratio has more than doubled. In East Boston and West Roxbury the dispersion measure increased 40 and 80 percent, respectively. Only in South Boston was there a very slight improvement in the measure. As will be discussed below, this may be attributed to the remarkable stability of South Boston during the ten years in question relative to the other subdivisions in question. Overall, the assessment inequalities observed by Oldman and Aaron in the early sixties worsened during the ten years since their study.

Tabulations for sixteen suburban towns are presented in Table 2-5. Although the assessment performance of jurisdictions in the suburban ring is considerably better than that for the city of Boston, a good deal of variation within jurisdictions still exists. The two worst

[d]Although the precise relationship between the ratio of standard deviation to mean and the coefficient of dispersion utilized by the Census Bureau depends on the distribution being examined and the number of observations in the sample, the coefficient of dispersion will almost always be a significantly smaller number.

suburban jurisdictions are actually rather similar to Boston. In Cambridge, with a mean ratio of .26 and a standard deviation of .18, nearly one-third of the units sold were either over- or underassessed by more than 69 percent: In Chelsea, the performance was hardly better with a mean of .29 and a standard deviation of .12.

A number of the towns with higher per capita incomes had rather good performances overall relative to Boston. Bedford, Belmont, Concord, Reading, Wakefield, Wellesley, and Melrose all had dispersion ratios (standard deviation divided by mean rates) of less than .16.

Tabulations for ten selected nonmetropolitan areas are presented in Table 2-6.[e] While the degree of intrajurisdictional variation changes significantly from site to site, the results present additional evidence of substantial inaccuracy of assessment.

[e]States were preselected to obtain a cross section of nonmetropolitan areas containing minorities. These data were originally gathered for use in a study of discrimination in nonmetropolitan housing markets under U.S. Department of Housing and Urban Development Contract H-2150-R. These tabulations were not used in that study.

Chapter 3

The Causes of Intrajurisdictional Rate Variations

Although the literature abounds with studies documenting the extent of intrajurisdictional inequalities in rates of property taxation, there has been only one major work dealing specifically with the causes of those inequalities. Oldman and Aaron state explicitly, "this study has revealed systematic inconsistencies in property tax assessment . . . explanations for this pattern are obscure"[1].

The only study that specifically attempts to deal with the question of causation is Black's 1969 study of Boston[2]. Black sets out to test three hypotheses about assessment behavior: (1) that assessment policy is "intentionally discriminatory with respect to certain cross sectional variables"; (2) that the assessor's only goal is to estimate accurately the market value of properties, that is, that errors are random; and (3) inequalities result from time lags in the assessment mechanism.

To test these hypotheses, Black uses Census tract data for the city of Boston and estimates a series of linear equations that explores the relationship between mean assessment sales ratios for each tract and the characteristics of those tracts. Not surprisingly, Black finds a systematic relationship between the assessment ratio prevalent in a tract and the general level of income, the percentage of nonwhite residents, and the percentage of properties in deteriorated condition. In addition, he finds that the rate of change of unit value in a tract exerts an influence on the assessment rate.

Unfortunately, while Black's results are interesting, they are consistent with all three of his hypotheses and shed little light on the question of causation. In conclusion, Black states:

> The findings of this study clearly identify assessment lags as an important cause of inequalities . . . another part of the total variation is explained by either or both of two hypotheses: inadvertent mis-estimation of market value and intentional tax rate discrimination. However, because the same general group of results support both hypotheses, it is impossible to determine to what extent either or both hypotheses are correct. Nevertheless, . . . some part of the total variation must be attributable to an assessment policy of deliberate tax discrimination[3].

No evidence is offered to support the final claim.

The present study is in part an attempt to deal more rigorously with the problem of causation. Broadly speaking, variation in assessment-sales ratios within jurisdictions must come from one of two sources: (1) randomness in selling price of a unit around its fair market value and (2) errors in estimating fair market value.

The present chapter will review current price theory and housing market theory to identify potential causes of randomness in selling price and potential sources of systematic assessment error. It will be argued that the search process that characterizes both the seller's and buyer's side of housing markets, as a result of imperfect information, implies that fair market value may be an illusory concept. What emerge from housing market interactions are sales prices that can be thought of as random draws from a price *distribution.* Such a market process by itself implies a certain randomness in *any* value estimation mechanism.

While Black suggests some of the potential sources of assessment error, there are a number of others. The sources to be discussed here and examined empirically in Chapter 4 using a number of data sets are: (1) errors resulting from incorrect housing market theory implicit in generally accepted assessing technologies; (2) errors resulting from changes in market values through time and infrequent updating; (3) errors resulting from simple inefficiency in the application of the generally accepted assessing technology; and (4) conscious over- and underassessment of properties.

The latter three sources of error are self-explanatory. The first involves an understanding of real estate price formation and will be dealt with here at some length.

IMPERFECT INFORMATION

From the first day of a course in principles, students of economics learn about equilibrium prices, which result from a market clearing process. The notion of a single prevailing market price for each commodity, however, is contradicted by even a casual glance through the advertisements in any daily newspaper. Examples of seemingly identical products selling for different prices in different locations abound. Gasoline pumped from the same tank truck can be seen selling for substantially different prices in the same city block. Drugs sold under brand names may sell for as much as ten or twenty *times* the price of the identical chemical compounds sold under their generic names.

The most commonly offered explanation for such observed price differentials is that the products themselves differ or are perceived to differ along one or more dimensions. When one buys a can of processed food, one takes a small risk of getting food poisoning. Since brand name processors face large pecuniary penalities if a consumer becomes ill, there are large incentives for such companies to insure proper health standards in processing. If there is, in fact, a lower probability of illness or a perceived lower probability, then inelasticity begins to creep into the demand curve facing the brand name, its goodwill acquires a capital value, and its price can be expected to diverge from the competitive price.

A second explanation for price differentials involves the somewhat ill-defined notion of transactions costs. This term has been used by various authors to refer to everything from the simple pecuniary cost of movement to and from the market to the cost of extensive negotiations that would be required to obtain production of public goods under a system of voluntary contribution[4]. While the precise meaning of transactions costs may vary from article to article, it clearly suggests a number of phenomena that are important determinants of market outcomes. Transactions costs in the traditional sense include most costs of engaging in exchange: transportation, time, disutility from shopping in an unpleasant or unsafe place, and so on. While most costs are well handled by the private market (through the retail sales industry or firms that produce transportation services), they may still result in different prices in different locations for seemingly identical products.

A third explanation for differing prices on similar commodities is market segmentation and price discrimination. It is trivial to demonstrate that if sellers possessed of market power can divide demanders into two or more identifiable groups that separately exhibit different demand elasticities, it will be optimal to charge different prices for each group.

A fourth explanation is that buyers and sellers possess imperfect information about product quality and prices. An extensive literature on market search germinated with a 1961 piece by Stigler[5]. Stigler postulates complete knowledge by buyers of the distribution of prices prevailing in the market but imcomplete knowledge of the location of specific prices. Consumers search for low prices (or high wages), paying the costs of search. Stigler does not posit any particular search pattern; he merely concludes that buyers will continue to search as long as the expected gain at the margin exceeds the marginal costs of continued search.

While the original model has been correctly criticized on a number of levels, extension of the model has corrected many of the problems and has led to a clearer understanding of the process as it exists in real world markets[6].

The most general and complete search model known to the author is presented in an unpublished work by Herman Leonard[7]. Leonard specifies a model in which both buyers and sellers search using uncertain information. Since his primary interest is in markets for housing, the model is one that assumes buyers seek to purchase only one unit of the commodity and that sellers have only one unit to sell. Buyers and sellers have prior experiences and acquire information in the process of search.

Leonard demonstrates rigorously that in any market for a homogeneous good where both buyers and sellers search according to predetermined decision rules "of practically any form"[8], there will emerge an equilibrium distribution of prices. He further demonstrates that if individuals with the same experience make differing choices regarding reservation price, the resulting equilibrium distribution will have a positive variance. This final condition will hold if (1) individuals have different search rules; (2) individuals have identical search rules but different search costs; or (3) individuals have identical search costs and decision rules but make errors in their calculations.

Although Leonard's model deals with the homogeneous goods case, he correctly points out that imperfections of information are likely to play an even more important role in markets for heterogeneous goods that differ along many dimensions. There is a prodigious amount of information required to accurately describe a good as complex as a housing unit. Given the relatively short time that most units remain on the market, it would be unreasonable to suspect that buyers are able to acquire and adequately assess all information available about a unit.[a] In addition, units also differ along

[a]A sample of 100 single family homes sold during 1971 and 1973 in the Boston Standard Metropolitan Statistical Area reveals that the average unit remained on the market for twenty-two days.

many unobservable dimensions requiring buyers to rely on available "signals"[9].

In any event, there is little doubt that much of the variation in housing prices observable within a metropolitan housing market is attributable to imperfect information on the part of buyers and sellers. The implication, then, is that even if assessors were in possession of complete information and if correct procedures were used to adjust for observable characteristics, the assessed price would be merely some function of an equilibrium price distribution and that the distribution of assessment-sales ratios would have a nonzero variance.

What is not clear is how much variation one would expect to result from this phenomenon. The answer would depend upon a large number of things. Examples include: (1) the presence or absence of informational intermediaries and their costs[10], (2) rate of turnover of properties, (3) the size of the market in units, (4) degree of informational exchange among sellers' agents,[b] and (5) structure of the existing transportation networks in the area.

Given the existence of equilibrium price distributions rather than equilibrium market prices, the definition of correct assessment becomes clouded. The assessment procedure itself implies the existence of a concept of fair market value for each property. If one thinks of selling price as a random variable, there are a variety of individual values that might be chosen as the proper fair market value. The most obvious candidates are the underlying mean, median, and mode. If the variation around fair market value is "normal," they are all the same, and the choice among them is immaterial.

If, however, distributions are skewed, the choice becomes more ambiguous. For example, some might argue that the mode is the correct underlying fair market value since it is the most likely value to emerge on any given draw. The appeal of the mean of the distribution as the definition of fair market value derives from the fact that it would minimize the sum of squared errors around fair market value. This fact has some significant merit on equity grounds. In addition, the mean represents the mathematical expectation or expected value of the property.[c] Again, on equity grounds one might argue that fair market value defined for tax purposes should be set

---

[b]For example, presence or absence of exclusive agent agreements or multiple listing services.

[c]The mean = $\int x f(x)\,dx$, essentially the probability weighted average selling price.

on the basis of what a property owner can expect to receive for the property were the owner to sell it.

If one accepts the mean of the equilibrium price distribution as the correct measure of fair market value or as the proper assessment, then the mean of any given sample is clearly the best estimator of that underlying value. The sample mean is the maximum likelihood estimator as well as being unbiased, consistent, and having the smallest variance among alternative estimators.

ERRORS IN ESTIMATING FAIR MARKET VALUE: INCORRECT ASSESSMENT TECHNOLOGY

Not all variation in observed effective rates of property taxation within jurisdictions can be attributed to randomness in selling price or imperfect markets. Even if a definition were agreed upon, there are a substantial number of potential sources of error in estimating fair market value. While some error may be the result of simple inefficiency in the application of currently accepted assessing techniques, assessors may err as a result of an incomplete or inaccurate understanding of the housing market.

This section will begin with a fairly detailed discussion of the nature of market prices of heterogeneous durable goods in general and housing more specifically. An attempt will be made to identify all factors that are likely to affect the value of an individual unit or a piece of real property. The section will conclude with a brief discussion of generally accepted assessing techniques and point to errors likely to result from their application.

The Determinants of Value

The problem of base valuation is complicated by the complexity of the real estate market and its sensitivity to external changes. The market value of an individual piece of real property at a given time is a function of a very large number of interrelated variables. This section of the book will outline a conceptual framework within which the analysis of property taxation will proceed. Its purpose is to serve as a benchmark against which generally accepted assessing procedures and results can be evaluated.

The traditional neoclassical approach to housing market analysis is to treat housing output as a single valued, homogeneous good: housing service. Housing service, however, is itself unobservable. By assuming that all housing inputs except land are variables in the long run and that housing markets adjust instantaneously to long-run equilibrium, it is possible to measure the quantity of housing services consumed by the households' expenditure on housing.

The most complete description of the traditional model is presented by Olsen (1969)[11]. Olsen defines a dwelling unit as a package composed of a capital asset called housing stock that yields some fixed amount of housing service per time period. The value of housing stock is derived from the long-run equilibrium price of housing service, which is uniform across the market. Thus, the value of an individual unit depends uniquely upon the quantity of housing stock that it contains. The housing stock in a particular unit may be increased or decreased through depreciation or investment. The concept of filtering derives from these notions. A unit is said to filter down when the quantity of housing stock that it contains is reduced, resulting in a lower yeild of housing services. Such a reduction may occur as a result of deterioration from lack of maintenance.

Such an approach obfuscates a number of extremely important dimensions of housing market operations and presents a very unclear picture of the formation of equilibrium property values. First, housing output is inadequately described in one dimension; it is extremely heterogeneous. Households obtain utility not from consuming some single-dimensioned service; rather, utility is obtained from the consumption of a large number of individually identifiable attributes. In choosing a residence, households choose simultaneously a number of rooms, a segment of land, a structure type, a set of neighbors, a package of local public services, and so on.

Presumably, traditional theorists assume that neighborhood attributes are part of housing stocks that yield services, and that changes in neighborhood characteristics that affect parcel values do so by changing the quantity of stock contained in them. More recent work by Polinsky and Shavell has extended the traditional model to include specific consideration of location-dependent amenities such as neighborhood characteristics[12]. Looking alternatively at a model of a closed and an open city, Polinsky and Shavell demonstrate that the effects of such variables on market value are extremely complex and can only be estimated in a general equilibrium context.

The Shavell-Polinsky model, however, still rests upon the assumption of long-run equilibrium. Casual observation indicates that housing capital stocks are durable and that supply responses are sluggish. Although a number of bundle components such as air conditioning, swimming pools, and so forth, may be added or altered on short notice, others such as room size are extremely difficult to change. Others, such as neighborhood composition, accessibility, and so one, are not even market produced. As a result, shifts in demand or changes in technology may result in positive or negative quasi-rents associated with specific geographic locations. The existence of such quasi-rents has been documented[13].

In order to understand the process of value formation, it is necessary to take explicit account of both the heterogeneity and durability of housing stocks. Individual units are really composite bundles of attributes. Housing attributes can be broken down into two major groups: structural characteristics $\{X\}$ and neighborhood characteristics $\{N\}$. In a sufficiently large area, a wide variety of alternative packages is available. Transactions are equivalent to tied sales. Although households observe only bundle prices, the availability of alternatives implies the existence of implicit prices associated with each bundle component. It is thus possible to represent equilibrium market value of a piece of residential property as a function of its attributes[14]. For purposes of illustration consider the simplest case, where there is no jointness in price determination and where the relationship is linear:

$$V = P_1 X_1 + \ldots P_m X_m + b_1 N_1 + \ldots b_n N_n \qquad (3\text{-}1)$$

where

V = Market price of bundle
P_i = Price of structural attribute i
X_i = Quantity of structural attribute i
b_i = Price of neighborhood attribute i
N_i = Quantity of neighborhood attribute i.

Each attribute price is made up of two components: a base price and a quasi-rent. That is,

$$P_i = (C_i + r_i) \qquad (3\text{-}2)$$

C_i = Construction cost of an additional
unit of attribute i
r_i = Quasi-rent associated with attribute i.

The r_i may be negative or positive and will persist only where the supply of the attribute in question is either fixed or responds sluggishly. Where quasi-rents are negative, supply response may be through depreciation, an obviously slow process. Where a particular attribute is in fixed supply, the entire return to that attribute is in the nature of a rent, that is, $C_i = 0$.

The nature of the b_i is somewhat different from the P_i since many of the N_i are not market produced and some may be in the nature of public goods. Some are not entirely fixed in the sense that production may take place through local government action or benefits to individual households may be reduced because of crowding or congestion: nevertheless, essentially all of the b_i can be considered in the nature of rents. The sum of the r_i and b_i can be thought of as the value of the land component exclusive of its value as a parcel of space.

Particularly unique neighborhood or locational characteristics are no different conceptually from any other attribute. If a particular piece of property happens to have a nice view, it will clearly sell for a higher price than an identical property with no view. Abstracting from jointness to be discussed below, the entire increment represents a return in the nature of a rent to the unique view. Within a clearly delineated market, there will be a single short-run equilibrium price associated with each attribute.

Thus far we have ignored two major conceptual problems that must be addressed before we proceed: first, the extent of market segmentation, and second, jointness in attribute price formation.

To illustrate the problem of market segmentation, let us begin with the polar case of two towns physicially separated from one another (no cross migration possible) and from the rest of the world, each with the same technologies and resources and a given housing stock. Assume that the incomes and tastes of the residents of Town A are similar to each other but quite different from those of the residents of Town B. One would expect to find very similar prices in Towns A and B associated with readily reproducible attributes but dissimilar prices on the nonreproducible attributes. The overall structure of attribute prices in each town would depend upon supply and demand forces particular to that town.

Housing markets are said to be segmented where separate demand or supply forces operate in separate portions of the market. Straszheim argues:

> Heterogeneity in the existing stock, other differences in neighborhood desirability, and the existence of discrimination imply that the urban housing market is, in fact, a set of compartmentalized and unique submarkets delineated by housing type and location[15].

Segmentation may result from income or taste differentials between various groups of housing demanders. There is a great deal of substitutability between homes in Wellesley and Weston (two high-income towns) or between homes in Everett and Malden, but very little at current prices between houses in Wellesley and those in Everett. As in the towns where no substitution was possible, the prices of readily reproducible attributes should equalize. Differentials in the structure of attribute prices can only result when supply response is sluggish or supplies are fixed. Here quasi-rents not only exist, but they also vary across submarkets.

A recent paper by Schnare and Struyk concludes that the prices of individual housing attributes do vary across submarkets but that the variation is small relative to the overall variation in attribute prices[16]. Their work, however, utilized a data base containing observations drawn from white middle- and upper-class neighborhoods. One would not predict much variation within such a homogeneous sample. However, the amount of variation in attribute prices between white and black submarkets or between very high and very low submarkets is considerable[17].

Equation (3-1) assumes that the relationship between the market value of an individual bundle and its component parts is a simple linear one with separate and independent attribute prices. However, the functional form of the actual relationship may be much more complex. Ideally the correct relationship should be derived from an underlying theoretical model. Unfortunately, there is nothing in the theoretical literature to provide anything but the most general guidance. Only one study to date has attempted to deal with the problem, and it provides no help whatsoever to housing market analysts[18]. What is clear is that the true relationship is complex because of a jointness in the determination of attribute prices. There is clear interaction between the various components of housing bundles that can be modeled in a variety of ways.

If it is assumed that capital markets are relatively free from major imperfections and that risk is properly evaluated, this framework is applicable to both owner-occupied and rental property. The value of any capital asset is equal to the present value of the net services that it is expected to yield through its lifetime. Owner-occupied housing yields, after allowance for depreciation, a flow of services for which owners implicitly pay a rent. Since there is no recordable transaction, such rents must be imputed from the value of homes. Rental property differs only in that two parties are involved and hence an explicit transaction must take place.

It should be noted, however, that the relationship between current rental flow and value is complicated. In urban areas where neighborhoods can change rapidly, one can observe widely divergent current rent to value ratios. If a neighborhood is expected to deteriorate, property values will fall to capitalize those expectations substantially before current rents begin to fall. Where expectations are volatile, the common practice of imputing market value from rental payments may be hazardous.

Commercial and industrial properties present an entirely different set of conceptual difficulties. Neighborhood or locational characteristics, including accessibility, generally become of primary importance. Parcel transactions are essentially land transactions. Improvements on industrial properties are generally firm or at least industry specific. As a result, commercial and industrial space is generally sold or rented by the square foot. Improvements are in the form of capital investment generally made at the time of initial occupancy and maintained or depreciated through time. Both here and with residential property, the legal distinction between real and personal property becomes critical. Generally, real property refers to fixed or permanent portions of the parcel. Some items of personal property (both tangible and intangible) are subject to taxation in thirty-eight states. In 1971 personal property represented 12.7 percent of the total assessed value of taxable property in the United States[19].

Changes in Value

It has been shown that parcels of real property may be viewed as bundles of structural and neighborhood attributes and that at any given time the market value of a property is a function of the quantity of the attributes that it possesses.

$$V_{it} = f(\widetilde{X}_t, \widetilde{N}_t) \tag{3-3}$$

where

V_{it} = Value of a parcel in submarket i at time t

$\widetilde{X}_t$ = Vector of its structural characteristics at time t

$\widetilde{N}_t$ = Vector of its neighborhood characteristics at time t

The partial derivatives of that function can be thought of as implicit market prices of the attributes; they will differ across submarkets.

$\widetilde{P}_{it} = \dfrac{\partial V_{it}}{\partial \widetilde{X}_t}$ = Vector of marginal structural attribute prices at time t in submarket i

$\widetilde{b}_{it} = \dfrac{\partial V_{it}}{\partial \widetilde{N}_t}$ = Vector of marginal neighborhood prices at time t in submarket i

In moving from time t to time $t + 1$, a number of variables may change, resulting in a change in the market value of the parcel:

1. The quantity of any of the structural attributes, $\tilde{X}$, may change.
2. The quantity of any of the neighborhood attributes, $\tilde{N}$, may change.
3. The submarket prices of either neighborhood or structural characteristics may change.

We shall discuss briefly the nature of such changes:
1. *The quantity of any of the structural attributes, $\tilde{X}$, may change.* Such changes occur through the processes of investment or physical depreciation either of a voluntary or involuntary nature. Some attributes are lumpy and may only be added or removed at discrete times. The owner of a property may add a room or a swimming pool or tear down a garage. Others are continuous or infinitely divisible such as quality or condition. Time, in the absence of continuous investment in the form of maintenance expenditures, results in a gradual reduction in a number of attributes that can be lumped under the headings of quality or condition.

The process of quality change due to physical depreciation has been discussed by a number of authors[20]. There is no question that the rate of depreciation and the rate of investment on general maintenance and repair are both critical elements on the supply side of the housing market. As such, they have been included as endogenous variables in the supply side of all the major urban simulation models[21].

Of particular concern for this book are two important facts. First, rates of physical depreciation will vary constantly across structure type and are by no means invariant with age or initial quality. Second, the rate of investment will depend on the implicit or explicit unexpected rate of return. The rate of return clearly depends upon a large number of factors including technology, patterns of demand, and money market conditions.

2. *The quantity of any of the neighborhood characteristics, $\tilde{N}$, may change.* This is perhaps the most interesting and, at the same time, the most complex set of intertemporal changes that affects the pattern of real property values.

At the simplest level are changes in the tax/public service package provided by local governments. Even here, however, the level of service perceived by consumers may be affected by a variety of factors other than simple expenditure levels. The outputs of public services that enter as an argument into individual utility functions are often difficult to define. Outputs such as the probability of being a victim of a crime or the actual transmission of cognitive skills in the classroom have been labeled C-outputs by Bradford, Malt, and Oates[22]. The unit cost of outputs defined in such a way depends upon a number of factors: (1) the effect of environment as an input into the productive process; (2) unit costs of inputs or intermediate goods such as police cars or teacher days; (3) the existence and extent of the congestion or crowding phenomena; and (4) economies of scale that might be realized in the productive process. Such factors may well vary extensively from jurisdiction to jurisdiction or even across neighborhoods within a given jurisdiction.

A second set of neighborhood characteristics that may change over time are the characteristics of the physical environment such as the level of air and noise pollution.

Finally, the general development of land use patterns and demographic trends are of critical importance and again operate by altering the dimensions of neighborhood quality or the quantity of various neighborhood attributes. For example, increased population density in an area will have a direct effect on the neighborhood environment as well as an indirect effect through a reduction of benefits per household that accrue from the public goods (both nationally and locally produced) subject to crowding. Certainly, the characteristics of the resident population may change through time and through migration. The process of neighborhood transition is extremely complex. Only the transition from all white to all black has received much analysis in the literature[23].

Neighborhood characteristics may also be subject to natural depreciation. The quality of roads, for example, if not maintained through periodic investment, will physically deteriorate. As in structural depreciation, rates may vary from neighborhood to neighborhood both with the age of the neighborhood and with the physical characteristics of the neighborhood.

The characteristics of individual neighborhoods are altered continuously by the location decisions of business firms. Such decisions directly affect the quality of the neighborhood or location and indirectly affect all neighborhoods by altering the pattern of employment or service accessibility. Both effects clearly depend critically upon the size and type of firm. A key decisionmaker, for example, will likely be followed by linked establishments and may result in a complete transformation in neighborhood character.

Accessibility to employment is a critical endogenous variable in virtually every existing theory of residential location and urban spacial structure[24]. In addition, a number of empirical studies have established its significance as a neighborhood attribute[25]. Since patterns of employment location are continuously changing, this dimension of neighborhood quality is critical if we are interested in patterns of property value changes through time.

One way in which communities have attempted to influence patterns of neighborhood change through time is with land use control legislation or zoning. Peterson has demonstrated empirically the importance of zoning as a determinant of property values[26]. Zoning may affect values either by directly regulating a number of important dimensions of neighborhood quality or by affecting expectations. Since expectations affect the price rather than the quantity of neighborhood attributes, they will be discussed in more detail below.

3. *The prices of either structural or neighborhood attributes, $\tilde{P}_{it}$ and $\tilde{b}_{it}$, may change.* The implicit prices of structural attributes have two components, a base price and a quasi-rent. The price attributes that are readily reproducible should approximate the current construction costs of the attribute with quasi-rents being zero or small. Where the attributes in question are more durable and difficult to alter, significant positive or negative quasi-rents may appear. In either case, changes in construction costs or technology can be expected to have an impact on attribute prices. If the cost of adding air conditioning equipment to an existing structure were to drop with the advance of solid state technology, the market value of a previously installed unit would be expected to drop.

A very significant portion of the value of the overall housing bundle, however, is made up of rents. They may be positive or negative quasi-rents associated with structural attributes that are durable or returns to scarce neighborhood attributes that are a portion of the land price. These price components are essentially demand determined and change in response to altered patterns of effective demand within the submarket.

Of particular importance in this regard is the role of expectations. Shifts in demand that result in increased land values and hence in increased rate of return are often anticipated. This is true especially since major shifts of demand are often caused by decisions of public bodies (zoning changes, highway construction), major private firms (location decisions of large firms), or developers. Gerard et al., in a study of Philadelphia, observe that the development of northern Philadelphia was anticipated early and capitalized into land values[27].

In general, the pattern of attribute prices that are essentially demand determined depends upon real incomes, tastes, and relative prices. Changes in any of the three factors can have a significant impact on land values.

Traditional Assessing Methods

Towns in the Commonwealth of Massachusetts systematically revalue all real property approximately every ten years. A telephone survey of twenty-six randomly selected towns in 1975 revealed that more than half (sixteen) had been revalued since 1969 and all but four had been revalued since 1964. There are two stages in nearly all revaluation programs, the majority of which are performed by outside contractors.

First, a door-to-door survey of each property is conducted. Fairly detailed information on the structural characteristics of each property is recorded on property record cards. Such cards usually contain rough floor plan sketches and condition and quality ratings as well as twenty to forty other pieces of information depending on the particular community.

Second, the information from the cards is used to assess the property, generally using the cost approach. Assessing associations and major contractors publish manuals for use by local assessors and revaluation field teams. These manuals generally contain detailed replacement cost data and depreciation factors for nearly all separate elements of the unit's construction. The value of increments in quality or condition is based on estimates of the dollar amount of investment needed to raise the rating.

While such a procedure is likely to prove accurate for estimating the value of characteristics that can be easily added to or removed from existing structures, it provides little guidance for valuing locational characteristics or characteristics whose values are in part made up of quasi-rents.

In nearly all cases, final assessments prepared by outside contractors are adjusted by the local assessors prior to implementation of the revaluation. In most New England towns, membership on the board of assessors is an elected position. Incumbent assessors tend to be reelected time after time with little difficulty. Assessors are usually individuals who have been or continue to be involved in the real estate market in some way. Most assessors are part-time city employees and are drawn heavily from the ranks of contractors, real estate agents, developers, or the like.

There is no question that assessors, particularly in smaller towns, have acquired a tremendous amount of information through time and that such information is used in making final assessments. What remains unclear is specifically what additional information is used and how it is used. It will be demonstrated in Chapter 5 that attempts to estimate intrajurisdictional tax capitalization effects suffer from substantial omitted variable bias. That is, there is a positive correlation between sales price and assessed value that is unexplained by the information contained on the property record card. One explanation offered is that assessors use information on observable characteristics also available to buyers that is not systematically recorded. Given the complexity of the housing bundle, this is not surprising. It is important to note that while neighborhood characteristics are rarely considered formally, there can be no doubt that assessors are aware of neighborhood value differentials. Chapter 5, pages 71 to 98, will explore empirically biases that result from the application of the traditional methods.

Chapter 4

The Causes of Intrajurisdictional Variations in Effective Rates: Three Empirical Analyses

As the preceding theoretical discussion suggests, variation in assessment-sales ratios can be caused by a number of things, and interpretations must be made with a good deal of caution. While a high level of observed variation may be indicative of poor assessing performance or bad assessing techniques, it may also be the result of substantial changes in the level or pattern of real property values or of a relatively unorganized set of market institutions.

This chapter will attempt to empirically sort out the causes of intrajurisdictional variation in tax rates. The chapter is comprised of three separate empirical studies: (1) a study of variation in the city of Boston, a jurisdiction that has made no real attempt to assess properties with any precision; (2) an analysis of assessment bias using micro data from fourteen jurisdictions that do exert considerable efforts to distribute the tax burden in proportion to property values; and (3) a study of the determinants of variation utilizing macro or aggregate data on a substantial number of Massachusetts cities and towns. This third analysis will attempt to separate factors that are likely to be affected by improved administration of the tax from those that are not.

THE CAUSES OF VARIATION WITHIN BOSTON

The data presented in Chapter 2 for the city of Boston reveal a very high average deviation around the mean assessment-sales ratio. For

33

the city as a whole, the standard deviation is larger than the mean assessment-sales ratio, indicating very large differentials in first-order effective tax rates among taxpayers.

To explain the observed variation in a particular jurisdiction, three items of information are required: (1) the basis for assignment of assessed values (the assessing technology), (2) the rate and pattern of correcting assessed values through time, and (3) the rate and pattern of changes in market values through time. In order to evaluate the assessing methods used by Boston's assessing department, it was necessary first to determine at precisely what time current assessments were made.

Historical documents of Boston's assessing department are stored in the basement boiler area of the East Boston District Court. For each property, documentation consists of eight items of information: (1) owner's name and address, (2) address of the property, (3) total area of the parcel, (4) total valuation, (5) valuation of the land, (6) valuation of the building, (7) the bill number, and (8) the total tax. Beyond this, no data are maintained on properties. Each property is listed annually and filed in alphabetical order by owner. No cross listings by address are available. Separate alphabetical listings are maintained for each of Boston's twenty-two wards.

While alphabetical listings by ward made it easy to trace properties that had not changed hands, it was more difficult to examine the prior assessments of properties that had been sold. It was initially decided to examine the period from 1960 to 1970, a period of substantial change in the city of Boston. Assessed values as listed in 1960 and 1970 were obtained for 440 properties that were held by the same owners in both years. The sample consisted of the first twenty such properties in each of the twenty-two alphabetical ward listings.

Out of 440 properties, 432 had the same assessment and identical breakdown (land/buildings) in both 1960 and 1970. Eight had assessments lowered, and none had assessments raised. Of the eight, seven had a lower building value and no change in land value; one had a lowered land valuation and a smaller area recorded.

Figures 4-1 and 4-2 are reproductions of single pages from the 1960 and 1969 listings of Ward 1.[a] Of the eight listings in 1969, six were held by the same owners in 1960. For none of the six was any change made in the file data or the assessment.

To check for the possible reassessment of properties upon sale, assessments in 1972 and 1975 were obtained for fifty properties

[a]The 1970 volumes were not available for reproduction.

sold during 1973.[b] In none of the fifty cases was the assessed value changed between those years.

The most significant piece of evidence was discovered by accident. Two employees of the assessing department claimed that assessments in Boston date to 1946. That year was also the last year that Boston listed its properties by street address. As a consequence it was possible to trace a substantial number of properties to their original assessments. A total of twenty-five properties were examined. In all cases there was no change in either valuation of land or buildings from the 1946 handwritten volumes to the 1973 computer listings on file in East Boston. Photocopies of records for four such properties in East Boston and Dorchester are included as Figures 4-3 through 4-8.

The 515 properties examined included commercial, industrial, single family, and multiple family residential. It can be stated with relative certainty that the Boston assessing office has made no systematic attempt to alter assessments in a great many years. It appears that, with a few exceptions, properties more than thirty years old were assessed in 1946 and that those assessments have not changed in thirty years.

Two kinds of information remain unclear: (1) how new properties were treated through time and (2) how assessments were made originally. An attempt was made to identify new properties among the 1973 sales; however, it was difficult, and no statistically significant pattern emerged. The Oldman and Aaron data reveal that commercial and multifamily rental properties are assessed at a high rate relative to the community norm[1]. To the extent that newer properties tend to fall heavily in these categories, one might infer that newer properties are assessed at a higher rate relative to true value than older properties. Much of the recent new construction in the city has been either major developments or large-scale projects.

Boston's assessing department maintains no public documentation of its assessing procedures. Since no data on structural characteristics of properties were available, it was impossible to directly infer the treatment of structural variables by the assessor from the assessments. An attempt will be made below (using aggregate data) to infer the assessor's treatment of neighborhood characteristics.

While the methods of initial assessment are unclear, once assessed values are established they change only rarely. As a consequence, changes in the pattern of assessment-sales ratios (and thus effective

[b]The 1973 *Real Estate Transfer Directory*, utilized in the assessment-sales ratio study in Chapter 2 lists both buyer and seller, facilitating the comparison.

THE COMMONWEALTH OF MASSACHUSETTS
CITY OF BOSTON
1969 ASSESSORS' REAL ESTATE VALUATION LIST

BILL NUMBER PARCEL NO.	NAMES AND RESIDENCES OF PERSONS ASSESSED (GIVE STREET AND NUMBER OF RESIDENCE) LOCATION	AREA	VALUATION			TOTAL TAX AND SPECIAL ASSESSMENTS, INCLUDING COMMITTED INTEREST			
			LAND (EXCLUSIVE OF BUILDINGS)	BUILDINGS (EXCLUSIVE OF LAND)	TOTAL OF EACH PARCEL OF REAL ESTATE	TAX	1968 UNPAID WATER LIEN AMOUNT	BETTERMENTS	UNPAID 1967 SEWER USE
07720 ① 4418-	C TRINGALE AND SONS INC 540R SUMNER 540R SUMNER	5833	1100	3900	5000	722 00			
07730 ② 4419-	C TRINGALE AND SONS INC 540 SUMNER VL SUMNER	131217	9400	00	9400	1357 36			
07735 ③ 4416-	C TRINGALE * SONS INC 14 JEFFRIES 14 JEFFRIES	90200	13500	12400	25900	3739 96			
07745 6061-	CACCAMESI CHARLES ASSUNTA CACCAMESI BE 198 LONDON 198 LONDON	1200	400	3600	4000	577 60			
07750 ④ 1514-	CACCAMESI PETER CARMELLA CACCAMESI BE 104 ST ANDREWS RD 104 ST ANDREWS RD 106 67 SEWER USE 735 104	4050	600	6100	6700	967 48			19 14
07760 ⑤ 5042-	CACCHIOTTI FRANK ANTONETTA CACCHIOTTI BE 19 LAMSON 19 LAMSON	1382	400	3300	3700	534 28			
07765 2109-	CACCHIOTTI ALFONSO ELLE CACCHIOTTI BE 76 BEACHVIEW RD 76 BEACHVIEW RD SS 862 60 STREET 103	4905	500	4500	5000	722 00		38 93	
07770 ⑥ 1343-	CACCHIOTTI ORAZIO LOUISE CACCHIOTTI BE 1046 SARATOGA 1046 SARATOGA VETERANS CREDIT 1046 NET TAX	3577	800	4200	5000	722 00 288 80 433 20			
		242364	26700	38000	64700	9342 68		38 93	19 14

ABATEMENT		STREET
NET TAX		SEWER
		SIDEWALK

THIS FORM APPROVED BY DEPARTMENT OF CORPORATIONS AND TAXATION

Figure 4-1.

101-1F—Dwellings
102-2F—(Write the
103-3F—Number of
104-4F—Families)
FAC—Factory

HOT—Hotel
IND—Industrial
MER—Mercantile
MILL—Mill
OFF—Office

STO—Stores
TAN—Tanks
THE—Theatre
S—Side of Street

1960 ASSESSORS' REAL ESTATE VALUATION LIST

Ward	Bill Number / Parcel No.	Names and Residences of Persons Assessed (Give Street and Number of Residence) Location	Area	Valuation: Land (Exclusive of Buildings)	Valuation: Buildings (Exclusive of Land)	Valuation: Buildings (See Legend)	Valuation: Total of Each Parcel of Real Estate	Total Tax and Special Assessments, Including Committed Interest: Tax	1959 Unpaid Water Lien Amount	Betterments
	107720 4418 ①	C TRINGALE AND SONS INC 540R SUMNER 540R SUMNER	5833	1100	3900		5000	50350		
	107730 4419 ②	C TRINGALE AND SONS INC 540 SUMNER VL SUMNER	131217	9400			9400	94658		
	107735 4416 ③	C TRINGALE & SONS INC 14 JEFFRIES 14 JEFFRIES	90400	13500	12400		25900	260813		
	107740 4758	CACARIELLO VINCENZO FILOMENA CACARIELLO 8 CHEEVER CT 8 CHEEVER CT S COR	1037	200	1800		2000	20140		
	107750 1514 ④	CACCAMESI PETER CARMELLA CACCAMESI SE 104 ST ANDREWS RD 104 ST ANDREWS RD 106	4050	600	6100		6700	67469		
	107760 5042 ⑤	CACCHIOTTE FRANK 19 LAMSON 19 LAMSON	1383	400	3300		3700	37259		
	107770 1343 ⑥	CACCHIOTTI ORANZIO 1046 SARATOGA 1046 SARATOGA	5577	800	4200		5000	50350		
		VETERANS CREDIT 1045 NET TAX						20140 30210		
	107780 2837	CACCIATORE RAIMONDO ANGELINE CACCIATORE SE 35 EUTAW 35 EUTAW	1875	600	2000		2600	26182		
	107790 7009	CACI BENIAMINO LARRISA CACI SE 205 PRINCETON 205 PRINCETON	1893	600	5100		5700	57399		
	107800 47	CACI BENJAMIN & ELISA 208 PRINCETON 208 PRINCETON	2233	1100	2200		3300	33231		
	107810 4734	CACISI MARIO J 166 WEBSTER 166 WEBSTER	5625	1700	4300		6000	60420		
			240922	30000	45300		75300	758271		

Figure 4–2.

THIS FORM APPROVED BY DEPARTMENT OF CORPORATIONS AND TAXATION

Assessors' Street Record
1946
City of Boston
PERSONAL ESTATE

Assessors' Street Record
1946
City of Boston
REAL ESTATE

Ward 16

Block No. 136

727

Figure 4-3.

THE COMMONWEALTH OF MASSACHUSETTS
CITY OF BOSTON
1973 ASSESSORS' REAL ESTATE VALUATION LIST

BILL NUMBER / PARCEL NO.	NAMES AND RESIDENCES OF PERSONS ASSESSED (GIVE STREET AND NUMBER OF RESIDENCE) / LOCATION	AREA	VALUATION LAND (EXCLUSIVE OF BUILDINGS)	BUILDINGS (EXCLUSIVE OF LAND)	TOTAL OF EACH PARCEL OF REAL ESTATE	TOTAL TAX AND SPECIAL ASSESSMENTS, INCLUDING COMMITTED INTEREST TAX	1972 UNPAID WATER LIEN AMOUNT	BETTERMENTS	UNPAID 1971 SEWER USE	
14500	FARMER JAMES L ETAL MARIE J FARMER BE 88 DIX 88 DIX	22								1
909-			9000	1800	3000	4800	944 16			
14510	FARNUM FREDERICK E ETAL JULIA F FARNUM FR3 16 RECTOR * WARDENS OF THE PARISH OF ALL SAINTS DORCHESTER FR10 16 PO BOX 599 195 ASHMONT 197	2								2
4753-			9777	9800	40200	50000	9835 00			3
14520	FARRELL CATHERINE T ETAL JOHN J FARRELL JT 184 MILTON 184 MILTON	24								
4562-			4248	600	4300	4900	963 83			4
14530	FARRELL GARRETT F ETAL ESTHER A FARRELL 53 AURIGA 53 AURIGA	22								5
1981-			6580	1300	4600	5900	1160 53			
14540	FARRELL JAMES A ETAL JULIA M FARRELL BE 30 FLORIDA 30 FLORIDA	24								6
1809-			4550	1300	3700	5000	983 50			
14550	FARRELL LUCY E 18 BELTON 18 BELTON	24								7
(2) 4594-			3203	500	4500	5000	983 50			
14560	FARRELL NORMAN J ETAL CAROLYN A FARRELL BE 45 WHITTEN	22								8
12710	DOWNING DENIS F ETAL MARY A DOWNING BE 3 ROSELAND 3 ROSELAND	22								5
1344-			2682	800	2700	3500	688 45			
12720	DOWNING JAMES E ETAL FLORENCE M DOWNING BE 10 BELTON 10 BELTON	24								6
(3) 4596-			3212	500	4500	5000	983 50			
	VETERANS CREDIT 10 NET TAX						393 40 590 10			7
12730	DOWNING JOSEPH J ETAL JOANNE DOWNING BE 14 SOUTH MUNROE TERR 14 SOUTH MUNROE TERR	22								8
2231-			4916	1100	5100	6200	1219 54			
12740	DOWNING WILLIAM H ETAL ELIZABETH H DOWNING BE 46 NAHANT AVE 46 NAHANT AVE	22								9
3817-			4125	400	3000	3400	668 78		23 55	
	67 SIDEWALK 110 51									10
										11
			31777	6700	35700	42400	8340 08		23 55	

		ABATEMENT		STREET	
		NET TAX		SEWER	
				SIDEWALK	

THIS FORM APPROVED BY DEPARTMENT OF CORPORATIONS AND TAXATION

Figure 4-4.

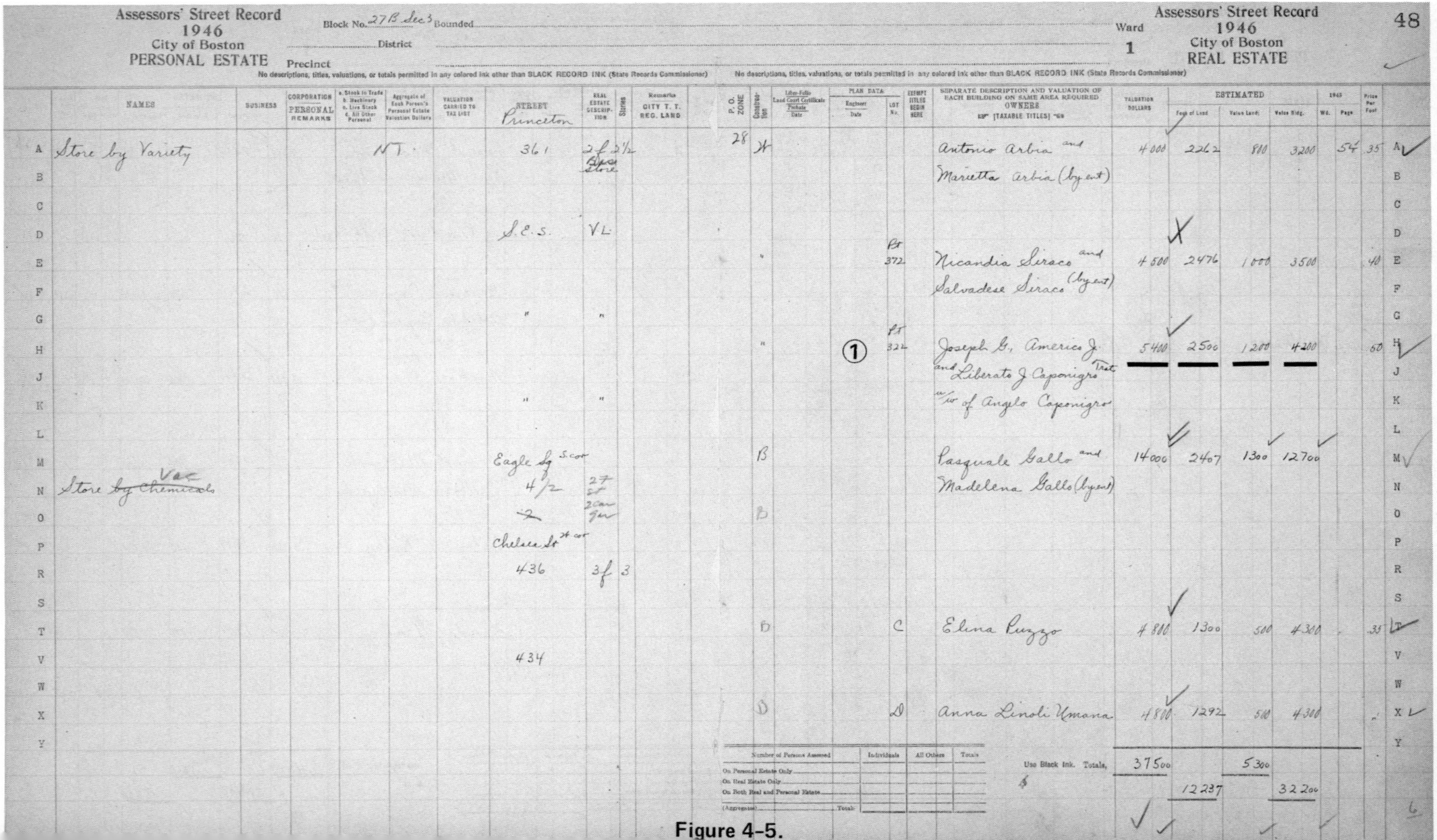

Assessors' Street Record 1946 City of Boston PERSONAL ESTATE — Block No. 27B Sec 3 Bounded — District — Precinct — Ward 1 — Assessors' Street Record 1946 City of Boston REAL ESTATE — 48

No descriptions, titles, valuations, or totals permitted in any colored ink other than BLACK RECORD INK (State Records Commissioner)

Line	Names	Aggregate of Each Person's Personal Estate	Street: Princeton	Real Estate Descrip-tion	P.O. Zone	Construc-tion	Plan Data	Lot No.	Owners	Valuation Dollars	Feet of Land	Value Land	Value Bldg.	Page	Price Per Foot	
A	Store by Variety	NT	361	2 f 2½ Bas Store	28	W			Antonio Arbia and	4000	2262	800	3200	54	.35	A
B									Marietta Arbia (by ent)							B
C																C
D			S.E.S.	VL												D
E						"		Pt 372	Nicandia Siraco and	4500	2476	1000	3500		.40	E
F									Salvadese Siraco (by ent)							F
G			"	"												G
H						"	①	Pt 324	Joseph G., Americo J.	5400	2500	1200	4200		.60	H
J									and Liberato J Caponigro Trst							J
K			"	"					u/w of Angelo Caponigro							K
L																L
M			Eagle Sq S cor			B			Pasquale Gallo and	14000	2407	1300	12700			M
N	Store by ~~Chemicals~~ Var		4/2	27 St					Madelena Gallo (by ent)							N
O			~~2~~	2 car Gar		B										O
P			Chelsea St N cor													P
R			436	3 f 3												R
S																S
T						B		C	Elina Ruzzo	4800	1300	500	4300		.35	T
V			434													V
W																W
X						D		D	Anna Linoli Umana	4800	1292	500	4300		"	X
Y																Y

Number of Persons Assessed	Individuals	All Others	Totals
On Personal Estate Only			
On Real Estate Only			
On Both Real and Personal Estate			
(Aggregate) Totals			

Use Black Ink. Totals: 37500 | 12237 | 5300 | 32200

Figure 4–5.

THE COMMONWEALTH OF MASSACHUSETTS
CITY OF BOSTON
1973 ASSESSORS' REAL ESTATE VALUATION LIST

NUMBER PEL NO.	NAMES AND RESIDENCES OF PERSONS ASSESSED (GIVE STREET AND NUMBER OF RESIDENCE) LOCATION	AREA	LAND (EXCLUSIVE OF BUILDINGS)	BUILDINGS (EXCLUSIVE OF LAND)	TOTAL OF EACH PARCEL OF REAL ESTATE	TAX	1972 UNPAID WATER LIEN AMOUNT	BETTERMENTS	UNPAID 1971 SEWER USE	
70	CAVALIERI FRANK ETAL JOSEPHINE CAVALIERI BE 7 CURTIS 28 7 CURTIS 11									1
0-	65 SIDEWALK 108 8	3240	2000	18300	20300	3993 01		7 56		
80	CAVALIERI JOSEPH A 30 DECATUR 28 30 DECATUR									2
4-		1200	600		600	118 02				
90	CAVALIERI JOSEPH A ETAL MARGARET CAVALIERI BE 28 DECATUR 28 28 DECATUR									3
5-	72 WATER 35014500-297-28 71 SEWER USE35014500-310-28	1190	600	2900	3500	688 45	60 00		12 95	4
00	CAVALIERI LORENZO F ETAL ANGELA M CAVALIERI BE 1148 BENNINGTON 28 1148 BENNINGTON									5
8-		3001	400	4300	4700	924 49				
10	CAVARRETTA FRANK J TRST CAV RLTY TRUST 478 SARATOGA 28 478 SARATOGA									6
2-		2500	1200	4200	5400	1062 18				
20	CAVICCHI JOHN ETAL LOUISE CAVICCHI BE 186 WORDSWORTH 28 25 BARNES AVE									7
9-	72 WATER 32122900-15-25 71 SEWER USE32122900-25-25	4781	900	5000	5900	1160 53	45 00		19 42	8
30	CAVICCHI JOSEPH 21 BARNES AVE 28 21 BARNES AVE									
8-	72 WATER 32122800-13-21 71 SEWER USE32122800-23-21	3942	800	1600	2400	472 08	30 00		5 40	9
										10
										11
		19854	6500	36300	42800	8418 76	135 00	7 56	37 77	

ABATEMENT		STREET	
NET TAX		SEWER	
		SIDEWALK	

THIS FORM APPROVED BY DEPARTMENT OF CORPORATIONS AND TAXATION

Figure 4-6.

Assessors' Street Record
1946
City of Boston
PERSONAL ESTATE

No descriptions, titles, valuations, or totals permitted in any colored ink other than BLACK RECORD INK (State Records Commissioner)

Block No. 2718 dos 3 Bounded ____ Southeasterly by Chelsea and Saratoga Sts.

District ____ Northwesterly by Princeton St.

Precinct ____

Assessors' Street Record
1946
City of Boston
REAL ESTATE

No descriptions, titles, valuations, or totals permitted in any colored ink other than BLACK RECORD INK (State Records Commissioner)

Ward 1

Figure 4-7.

THE COMMONWEALTH OF MASSACHUSETTS
CITY OF BOSTON
1973 ASSESSORS' REAL ESTATE VALUATION LIST

NAMES AND RESIDENCES OF PERSONS ASSESSED (GIVE STREET AND NUMBER OF RESIDENCE) LOCATION	AREA	VALUATION LAND (EXCLUSIVE OF BUILDINGS)	BUILDINGS (EXCLUSIVE OF LAND)	TOTAL OF EACH PARCEL OF REAL ESTATE	TAX	1972 UNPAID WATER LIEN AMOUNT	BETTERMENTS	UNPAID 1971 SEWER USE
50 CIAMPA JAMES ETAL MATTEO LOCONTE TC 269 MERIDIAN 28 269 MERIDIAN 271 SECOR	1078	3200	4800	8000	1573 60			
60 CIAMPA JOSEPH J ETAL ANTONIETTA CIAMPA BE 27 MORRIS 28 101 MORRIS	1500	400	3500	3900	767 13			
70 CIAMPA JOSEPH M ETAL ANTONETTA CIAMPA 80 WORDSWORTH 28 80 WORDSWORTH	2500	500	2000	2500	491 75			
VETERANS CREDIT 80 NET TAX 65 SIDEWALK 108 29					393 40 98 35		8 10	
80 CIAMPA MARIA 62 BREMEN 28 62 BREMEN	2127	600	3600	4200	826 14			
90 CIAMPA MARY ETAL ALBERT CIAMPA FR 2 17 MURRAY CT 28 17 MURRAY CT	1296	300	1600	1900	373 73	30 00		
72 WATER 30064200-756-17 71 SEWER USE30064200-754-17								7 55
00 CIAMPA PASQUELINA LT JOSEPH & MICHAEL CIAMPA REM 347 PRINCETON 28 347 PRINCETON	2200	600	2300	2900	570 43			
0 CIAMPA PELLEGRINO 951 REVERE BCH PKWY 51 72 LIVERPOOL	1600	800	3000	3800	747 46			
0 CIAMPA PELLEGRINO 951 REVERE BCH PKWY 51 LIVERPOOL NWNCOR COPPERSMITH WAY NE	1400	700		700	137 69			
	13701	7100	20800	27900	5487 93	30 00	8 10	7 55
ABATEMENT						STREET		
NET TAX						SEWER		
						SIDEWALK		

THIS FORM APPROVED BY DEPARTMENT OF CORPORATIONS AND TAXATION

Figure 4-8.

tax rates) that occur through time must be attributed largely to changing patterns of real estate values. Defining the progressivity of the property tax in terms of its own base, the tax will become more regressive through time if higher valued properties appreciate faster than lower valued properties. Conversely, if lower valued properties appreciate faster than higher valued properties, the tax will move in the direction of progressivity.

While the fact that assessed values have not changed in many years is suggestive of simple inefficiency; there is no evidence to reject the hypothesis that this inertia represents a carefully calculated policy. Since it results from specific actions (or lack thereof) by the city officials, it can be thought of as city policy by definition. The remaining portion of this section will examine changes in Boston neighborhoods through time and attempt to link them with observed changes in first-order effective tax rates.

Effective Rate Changes 1950–1960 and Initial Assessment Bias

In order to examine the impact of changes in the pattern of real estate values on effective tax rates, it was decided to use the community as the unit of observation. Boston is composed of eight relatively homogeneous communities from which sales data were available.[c] While significant changes have taken place in some, others have remained remarkably stable through time. Census tract data were aggregated to obtain housing and population characteristics for each community in 1950, 1960, and 1970.[d]

In Table 4-1, census data on changes in rents and values between 1950 and 1960 were used to impute assessment-sales ratios for 1946. The average increase in residential property value between 1950 and 1960 was estimated by taking an average of the percentage change in median contract rent and the percentage change in the median value of owner-occupied housing weighted by the percentage of units in each community that are owner occupied. This factor was multiplied by 1.4, assuming that rent and value increases from 1946 to 1950 were at the same rate as those from 1950 to 1960.[e]

[c]Brighton, Charlestown, Dorchester, East Boston, Hyde Park, Roxbury, South Boston, and West Roxbury.

[d]See appendix. Weighted averages were used where simple summation was impossible (i.e., median income).

[e]It could be argued that the rate of increase in rents should not be used since their impact on the values of rental property depends upon expectations. When expectations are not favorable, rent-value ratios are low. When expectations are favorable, rent-value ratios are high.

Table 4-1.   Estimated Mean Assessment-Sales Ratios for 1946, Boston

	(1) Mean Assessment-Sales Ratio 1960–1962 Sales[a]	(2) Δ in Median Contract Rent 1950–1960[b]	(3) Percent Owner Occupied[b]	(4) Δ in Median Value of Owner Occupied 1950–1960[b]	(5) Estimated Change in Residential Property Values 1950–1960[c]	(6) Estimated Assessment-Sales Ratio 1946[d]
Brighton	.38	.71	.18	.35	.64	.87
Charlestown	.54	.56	.30	.57	.56	1.17
Dorchester	.43	.71	.25	.31	.61	.95
East Boston	.44	.68	.28	.39	.60	.99
Hyde Park	.32	.76	.53	.39	.56	.70
Roxbury	.65	.49	.13	.40	.47	1.33
South Boston	.47	.53	.24	.62	.55	1.01
West Roxbury	.33	.57	.65	.37	.44	.67
Total[e]	.45	.62	.27	.42	.56	.99

[a] See Chapter 2 and Oldman and Aaron op. cit.
[b] See Appendix.
[c] [(Column 2) X (1 – Column 3) + (Column 3) X (Column 4)].
[d] [(Column 5 + 1) X (Column 1)] X 1.4.
[e] Totals are averages weighted by number of housing units in 1950.

Overall for Boston, it was estimated that residential property values rose approximately 56 percent between 1950 and 1960. Rents rose at 62 percent and owner-occupied unit values 42 percent. An overall assessment-sales ratio of .45 in 1961 is consistent with the hypothesis that assessments in 1946 were made at an average of 100 percent. The estimated 1946 mean assessment-sales ratio under the above assumptions is .99.

While value changes through time explain fully changes in the level of assessment, they are insufficient to explain the pattern of assessments across the eight communities. Roxbury, for example, in 1961 was assessed at about twice the rate of Hyde Park and West Roxbury. While rent levels in Roxbury rose at a slower rate than in any other community between 1950 and 1960, rents in general rose faster than house values. Since Roxbury is 87 percent rental property, its overall estimated rate of increase in values (Column 5 on Table 4-1) was not significantly different from the corresponding rate for other communities. The estimated assessment rate for Roxbury in 1946 is nearly twice as high as the corresponding rates for West Roxbury and Hyde Park[2].

It should be noted that the data reveal a very significant amount of variation in assessment rates within each of the eight communities. As such, the estimates presented here are subject to considerable error. By dealing with mean assessment-sales ratios, however, we are able to reduce the expected error by a factor of $1/\sqrt{N}$ where N is the number of sampled sales in each community.

Casual observation of the results presented in Table 4-1 reveals that the variation in estimated assessment rates for 1946 is not random across communities. The two communities that seem to have been significantly underassessed are Hyde Park and West Roxbury. These two communities are the only ones with predominantly single family housing stocks. The most significantly overassessed community is Roxbury, which has the smallest percentage of owner-occupied stock and the lowest income levels among the eight.

Table 4-2 presents rank order comparisons of the estimated assessment rate and community characteristics in 1950. The coefficient of correlation between the assessment rate and income level is .84. Assessment and value have a correlation coefficient of .79. Assessment and percentage of owner-occupied housing have a correlation coefficient of .78.

Using ordinary least squares, the parameters of the following model were estimated:

$$A = \beta_0 + \beta_1 VAL + \beta_2 OWN + \beta_3 BLACK + e \qquad (4\text{-}1)$$

Table 4-2. Rank Order Comparisons of Community Characteristics and Assessment Rates

	Estimated Assessment Rate 1946[a]	Median Income 1950[b]	Median Value Owner-Occupied Housing 1950[b]	Percent Owner Occupied 1950	Median Contract Rent 1950[b]
West Roxbury	.67	4,300	12,400	65	60
Hyde Park	.70	3,300	9,300	53	33
Brighton	.87	3,400	10,700	18	45
Dorchester	.95	3,200	9,800	25	38
East Boston	.99	2,700	5,700	28	25
South Boston	1.01	2,900	5,300	24	31
Charlestown	1.17	2,500	4,300	30	27
Roxbury	1.33	2,500	5,768	13	33

[a]See Table 4-1.
[b]See Appendix.

where

A = Estimated assessment rate, 1946
VAL = Median value of owner-occupied housing in 1950 (in thousands)
OWN = Percent owner-occupied housing, 1950
$BLACK$ = Percent of population that is black, 1950 (is essentially a dummy variable for Roxbury).

Income and rent level were excluded because of the high level of colinearity among value, rent, and income. Pairwise correlation coefficients among the three factors range between .87 and .93. Results of the estimation reveal that all three independent variables are significant:

$$A = 1.3 + 0.019\ BLACK - 0.0044\ OWN - 0.035\ VAL$$
$$\quad (14.1)\ (2.7) \qquad\qquad (2.1) \qquad\qquad (3.0) \qquad (4\text{-}2)$$
$$\overline{R}^2 = .88$$

Durbin Watson Statistic = 1.7

Figures in parentheses are t-statistics. 5 percent critical value for a 1 tailed t-test (4 d.f.) is 2.1.

Three conclusions emerge about initial assessment patterns. First, Boston assessors seem to have initially assessed higher value properties in higher income areas at lower than average rates. Second, assessors seem to have assessed owner-occupied housing units at lower than average rates. Finally, when assessment variations attributable to value level and stock composition are controlled for, Roxbury remains overassessed relative to other communities.

While this analysis is suggestive of the patterns of bias that appear to have been present in 1946 when assignment of assessed values was first made in Boston, the explanation for their existence remains unclear. There are a number of interesting scenarios consistent with the evidence presented. Other portions of this study are concerned primarily with error by assessors who are indeed attempting to estimate fair market values. Two alternative explanations or partial explanations merit further study: (1) tax assessment patterns derive from social structure and political considerations and (2) tax rate patterns across the jurisdiction are in part determined by the pattern of expenditures and service provision across the jurisdiction[3].

Boston is today and was in 1946 a fascinating mixture of segregated and politically active racial and ethnic groups, particularly Irish and Italian. The relationship between the assessing department and its behavior and the political concerns of successive city administrations would make a fascinating study. Another interesting project would be to attempt to allocate expenditure benefits geographically and relate them through time with the tax rate distributions presented here.

Effective Rate Changes 1960-1973
Chapter 2 presents observed mean assessment-sales ratios by community for both 1960 to 1962 and for 1973. As a consequence, it is possible to obtain a more accurate picture of the impacts of neighborhood changes on effective tax rates using data from this later period.

Table 4-3 presents changes in values, rents, and assessment ratios during the 1960s. The most significant changes in Boston during that period took place in Charlestown and Dorchester.

Dorchester began to tip during the late sixties, going from virtually all white to 24 percent black in a short time. Median income fell significantly relative to the Boston average. At the same time, both rents and values increased at the slowest rates among the eight communities.

A weighted average of the change in values and the change in rent levels suggests an average increase in residential values of 35 percent

Table 4-3. Changes in Value, Rent, and Assessment-Sales Ratios, 1960-1970, Boston

	(1) Δ in Mean Assessment Sales Ratio 1960-1973[a]	(2) Δ Median Value of Owner Occupied 1960-1970[b]	(3) Δ Median Contract Rent 1960-1970[b]	(4) Estimated Δ in Residential Property Value 1960-1970[c]
Brighton	-.33	.51	.70	.67
Charlestown	-.61	.82	.74	.76
Dorchester	-.19	.21	.40	.35
East Boston	-.46	.49	.57	.55
Hyde Park	-.37	.47	.72	.59
Roxbury	-.43	.35	.74	.69
South Boston	-.60	.47	.62	.58
West Roxbury	-.39	.45	.41	.44
Total[d]	.37	.40	.60	.55

[a]See Chapter 2 and Oldman and Aaron *op. cit.*
[b]See Appendix.
[c]Average of Columns (2) and (3) weighted by 1970 percent owner occupied.
[d]Totals are averages weighted by 1970 total housing units.

for Dorchester. Such an increase would predict a 35 percent decline in the mean assessment-sales ratio, everything else being constant. The actual decline, however, was only 19 percent, suggesting that values increased by only 19 percent. Such an increase is quite consistent with the 21 percent change in the value of owner-occupied housing. Clearly, using changes in rent levels as a proxy for changes in the capital value of rental housing significantly overstates the change in values in a declining area. There is no question that rent-value ratios fell significantly in Dorchester during the period. Thus, the 19 percent decline in assessment rates may be perfectly consistent with the observed neighborhood changes under the assumption that assessed values remained unchanged.

While values and rents in Roxbury did much better during the period overall, the same discrepancy between rent levels and values is evident. In both Roxbury and Dorchester, rents rose twice as fast as values of owner-occupied housing units. Again, if uncertainty or unfavorable expectations caused a rise in rent-value ratios for individual buildings, the rates of increase in single unit value (0.35) and rents (0.74) may be consistent with the rate of property value increase implied by the change in assessment rate (0.43).

This same problem may be true for Boston as a whole. Using a weighted average of rent and owner-occupied value changes to estimate the overall change in residential values yields a higher figure (0.55) than the change in assessment rates would predict (0.37). The weighted mean change in the value of owner-occupied housing (0.40) is much more consistent with such a change. Once again, if rent-value ratios for the city as a whole were rising as the result of unfavorable expectations, these numbers would be fully consistent. This may not be an unreasonable assumption given the crime, fiscal, and racial problems (including busing) experienced by Boston as well as other Northern industrial central cities during the late sixties and early seventies.

Charlestown experienced the most rapid rise in values as well as in rental levels. While the assessment-sales ratio fell in Charlestown more than in any of the other seven communities, it only fell 61 percent while rents rose 74 percent and values 82 percent. While no hard evidence is presented here, it may well be that a significant amount of old low-valued stock was cleared or a significant amount of new construction assessed at a higher rate than the older properties took place during the period. A similar scenario may explain the smaller than expected fall in assessment-sales ratios in Brighton and Hyde Park. All three communities experienced large changes in number of housing units. In Charlestown, the stock fell by 20 percent net. In

Brighton and Hyde Park the number of housing units increased by 15 percent and 12 percent, respectively.[f]

In the more stable communities of South Boston and West Roxbury, the weighted average of rent and value increases explains the fall in assessment ratios precisely. In East Boston the weighted average does only slightly less well.

In sum, the most salient feature of Boston's assessing department is inertia. Changes in individual neighborhoods or communities are sufficient to explain changes in the pattern and level of assessment rates that took place during the 1960s. Such changes are sufficient to explain the mean level of assessment in 1960, assuming a 100 percent mean rate in 1946. Rent and value changes are, however, insufficient to explain the pattern of assessment ratios in 1960. There is significant evidence that original assessments were made at a lower than average rate on high-value properties and on owner-occupied units. There is also evidence that Roxbury was originally overassessed even when discounting for the small percentage of owner-occupied housing and for the low value of the stock.

THE CAUSES OF VARIATION IN TOWNS
WITH GOOD PERFORMANCE

Boston is not typical of taxing jurisdictions. The data in Chapter 2 reveal that most jurisdictions exhibit significantly less variation in assessment rates and effective tax rates. This section will examine the causes of rate variation within jurisdictions with the so-called best performance. Using micro data on a large number of individual housing units that were sold in the past few years, an attempt will be made to explain observed assessment errors by noting their relationship to both the structural and neighborhood characteristics of the unit.

The discussion in Chapter 3 of traditional assessing technology based on replacement costs predicts that assessors will err in their consideration of neighborhood attributes and in valuing structural characteristics that cannot easily be altered on existing units.

The Data

Two data sets were used in the empirical work to follow. The first contains observations on 2,195 single family homes located in thirteen predominantly white suburban Boston communities sold during 1971. The second contains observations on 1,084 single

[f]See appendix.

Table 4-4.   Income and House Value by Community

Community	Median Income High Tract	Median Income Low Tract	Weighted Median	Sample Mean House Value
Arlington	15,963	11,286	14,321	30,042
Bedford	16,610	14,594	15,756	37,095
Belmont	24,771	12,006	17,752	46,356
Concord	23,378	17,995	20,898	49,134
Lincoln	27,635	27,635	27,635	62,766
Melrose	17,515	12,393	14,255	28,012
Reading	33,708	13,133	15,092	31,752
Saugus	13,279	11,723	12,360	24,713
Stoneham	15,114	11,603	13,300	28,513
Wakefield	15,749	12,452	13,908	29,029
Waltham	13,966	9,518	12,723	28,698
Wellesley	26,250	19,074	22,755	49,497
Weston	33,708	13,133	29,250	60,934

family units sold between 1972 and 1975 in Hanford, California.

The Boston Data. Transaction prices on the Boston homes were obtained from the *Real Estate Transfer Directory* published by a local firm.[g] Care was taken to include only "arm's length" sales, data were obtained on all 1971 sales of single family units in each of thirteen municipalities.

The municipalities chosen are all primarily residential communities located within two closely linked housing market areas. Eight of the thirteen are middle-income communities located in the north and inner west ring. The remaining five are upper-income communities in the outer northwestern ring. Table 4-4 contains data on income by census tract and mean sales price for the sample.

The primary reason for choosing this particular sample of cities was availability of data. Assessors in this particular group of municipalities maintained exceptional records of property characteristics. It is thus not surprising that assessing performance in these cities as measured by the coefficient of dispersion around the mean assessment-sales ratio is superior to other areas discussed in Chapter 2.

Despite this nonrandom selection procedure, the sample is a reasonably representative cross section of Boston suburban communities. Table 4-5 compares the income distribution for the tracts in the sample with all tracts in the suburban ring and in the Standard Metropolitan Statistical Area (SMSA).

The structural characteristics of the properties were obtained from property record cards on file at the thirteen local assessors' offices in

[g]See discussion of Chapter 2.

Table 4-5.   Distribution of Money Income: Average Tract Income

(000's)	Sample	Suburbs	SMSA
0-7.0	0	0.1	1.2
8-9.9	0.3	2.8	3.8
10-11.9	6.0	18.8	21.1
12-13.9	33.3	27.5	26.7
14-15.9	18.7	21.2	20.2
16-17.9	12.0	11.2	10.2
18-19.9	4.5	16.4	5.8
> 20	25.1	12.3	11.3

Source: U.S. Department of Commerce, Bureau of the Census, 1970 Census of Population and Housing, *Census Tracts.*

each municipality. While selling prices and assessed values are publicly recorded, the property record card is not considered a public document in the Commonwealth of Massachusetts. As such, the cooperation of each assessor had to be obtained individually.

Information on fifteen structural and lot characteristics was obtained on each unit and recorded on IBM coding forms. In addition, documentation on such items as condition codes was obtained. All variables were constructed to insure consistency across towns.

Each unit in the sample was assigned to a census tract using street address and a census coding workbook. Several tract characteristics from the 1970 Census of Population and Housing were used as neighborhood descriptors, including income, density, proportion "low status" and black, number of vacant units, and so on.

Fiscal data were obtained from several sources including the Massachusetts Department of Corporations and Taxation, Bureau of Local Assessment, and the Massachusetts Department of Commerce.

Finally, accessibility was proxied with a gravity index. The access variable is basically a weighted average of the straight line distances between the tract and five employment centers in the Boston SMSA.

Tables 4-6a and 4-6b present the neighborhood and structural variables used in the analysis and give summary statistics describing their variation within the sample.

The California Data.   The data from Hanford, California, consist of 1,084 observations on single family homes sold within a single fiscal jurisdiction.[h] Hanford, with a 1970 population of 15,179, is

[h]These data were used in a study of housing discrimination prepared for the U.S. Department of Housing and Urban Development by the author. Data were collected and prepared under the supervision of the author.

Table 4-6a. Massachusetts Data: Structural Characteristics, *N* = 2195

	Mean	*Standard Deviation*	*Minimum*	*Maximum*
Price	37,512	17,526	10,000	165,000
Assessed Value	25,827	13,489	1,000	106,470
Lot Size (sq. ft.)	17,984	23,171	1,086	523,590
Floor Space (sq. ft.)	1,491	746	270	9,000
Rooms (no.)	6.8	1.70	3	18
Quality (1 = best)	4.6	1.80	1	9
Year Built (1900 or earlier = 0)	42.6	21.20	0	71
Baths (no.)	1.6	.73	1	6
Fireplaces (no.)	1.0	.84	0	8

	Percent of Units with
Modern Kitchen	31
Full Basement	94
Brick or Stone Face	5
One-Car Garage	41
Two-Car Garage	32
Two-Car Garage	1
Central Air	1
Built-in Pool	1

located in central California about thirty miles south of Fresno. It is a rapidly growing city with a population growth of 33 percent from 1960 to 1970.

The data are similar to the Massachusetts data but are more complete and consistent since they were obtained from a single jurisdiction. Information on eighteen structural characteristics was obtained from the local assessor on each of the individual units sold between 1972 and 1975.[i]

Research assistants on site in the town of Hanford divided the city into twenty-nine individual neighborhoods. Each neighborhood was assigned a subjective condition rating from 1 to 10 based on general condition of the roads, structures, street lighting, and so forth. The code was assigned independently by two individuals and an average was computed. Access is an index of the linear distance from the center of the neighborhood to the central business district.

Of the recorded transactions, 1,014 were obtained from fifteen of the twenty-nine neighborhoods. The analysis below will focus on this

---

[i]Local taxing jurisdictions in California have been under state pressure to update and maintain accurate records and to employ efficient assessing procedures. Property record cards were in excellent condition.

Table 4-6b. Massachusetts Data: Neighborhood Characteristics

	Mean	Standard Deviation	Minimum	Maximum
Access[a]	1.5	.27	.95	1.99
Income[b]	17,103	5,356	9,518	33,708
Per Pupil Expenditures[c]	886	199	644	1422
Nominal Tax Rate[d]	55	25	33.5	121.6
Full Value Tax Rate[d]	42.3	3.89	35	48
Population Density[b]	3,783	2,744	520	10,333
Percent Single Family[b]	74	20	4	97
Percent Low Status[b,e]	7	4	3	30
Percent Black[b]	0	0	0	4
Percent Vacant Units[b]	1	1	0	5

[a] Access is constructed as follows:

$$Ln\ (DISTANCE)\ t = Ln\ (a_1 X_{1t} + a_2 X_{2t} \cdots a_5 X_{5t})$$

where X_{it} is the straight-line distance between the tract and the ith employment center, and a_i is the proportion of total SMSA manufacturing wholesale, retail, and service employment contained in that center. The five centers were Boston, Cambridge, Lynn, Quincy, and Waltham.

[b] Department of Commerce, Bureau of the Census, *1970 Census of Population and Housing, Census Tracts, Boston.*

[c] Integrated expenditure per pupil in regular day, special, vocational day classes including administration, instruction health, transportation, rental of land and buildings, maintenance of plant, and other sundry functions. Reproduced in *Universal Atlas of Metropolitan Boston*, Universal Publishing Co., 1972.

[d] Tax rates obtained from local assessment bureau, Department of Corporations and Taxation, Commonwealth of Massachusetts.

[e] Low Status = .5 · (fraction of males with less than 8 years of school plus the fraction of males employed as laborers).

subsample. The remaining fourteen neighborhoods contained an average of five transactions each and were excluded from the neighborhood portion of the analysis. Sales prices of units sold were on file at the assessor's office. Table 4-7 presents summary statistics for the data.

The Model

In order to make some inferences about how assessors finally arrive at assessed values and to identify sources of error, the parameters of the following model were estimated using Massachusetts and California data:

$$(SP - AV/\overline{AR}) = \beta_0 + \sum_i \beta_i x_i \qquad (4\text{-}3)$$

Table 4-7. California Data, *N* = 1084

	Mean	Standard Deviation	Minimum	Maximum
Selling Price	22,795	9,550	2,360	77,625
Assessed Value	22,352	10,115	3,000	85,000
Lot Size (code 1 = smallest)	2.03	.56	1	5
Floor Space (sq. ft.)	1,291	375	110	4,830
Rooms (no.)	5.4	.93	1	9
Quality (code 8 = best)	5.5	.84	2	8
Year Built (1900 or earlier = 0)	55.9	18.8	0	75
Baths (no.)	1.6	.47	1	3.5
Fireplaces (no.)	.54	.52	0	2
Garages (no.)	.88	.32	0	2
Condition Overall (9 = best)	6.3	2.1	1	9
Construction (ranked type 9 = best)	3.9	.55	0	9
Condition Exterior (3 = best)	.84	.40	0	3
Heating (1 = best)	2.8	1.6	0	5
NHBD Quality (9 = best)	7.1	1.8	2	9
Access	72.3	25.1	20	135
NHBD Assessment-Sales Ratio	.96	.08	.79	1.08

	Percent of Units
With Full Basement	1.5
With Swim Pool	5.8
With Air Conditioning	66.9
On Sewer Tie-in	98.8
With Modern Kitchen	99.7
On Paved Road	99.7
In Black Neighborhoods	3.1
In Mexican Neighborhoods	10.9

Source: Assessing Office, Kings County Courthouse, Hanford, Ca.

where

SP = Sales price

AV = Assessed value

$\overline{AR}$ = Mean assessment-sales ratio for the jurisdiction

x_i = Unit or neighborhood characteristic i.

The model is designed to indentify characteristics that were not considered by the assessor or that were improperly valued.[j] The dependent variable is an estimate of the assessment error. The model attempts to identify the systematic component of that error. A positive and significant $\hat{\beta}_i$ implies that the assessor is ignoring or undervaluing a characteristic, i, that has a positive influence on market value or that the assessor is overestimating the influence of a so-called negative characteristic. A negative and significant $\hat{\beta}_i$ indicates overvaluation of a so-called positive characteristic or undervaluation of a negative characteristic. Since fluctuation in market value due to imperfect information, and so on, should be random with mean zero, the observed assessment error caused by such fluctuation should be independent of the xs and should have no influence on the estimated βs.

Since the California data contain more detail in individual neighborhoods within the jurisdiction, a more detailed analysis was possible with those data. The results are presented in Table 4–8. Two specifications of the model were utilized. In the first, six specific neighborhood characteristics were included. In the second, they were replaced with dummy variables for fourteen of the fifteen neighborhoods from which a significant sample of sales was drawn.

The Results

There are a number of interesting results. First, none of the structural characteristics that can be easily modified appears significant in either specification. Adding air conditioning, a swimming pool, a garage, or a finished basement generally involves no major structural modifications. As a consequence, economic theory predicts that construction costs and market price should be very close; there should be no quasi-rents associated with these particular characteristics. Since the assessment procedure rests on a construction cost foundation, one would anticipate accurate assessment and thus predict insignificant coefficients on these variables.

For similar reasons but to a lesser extent, one might expect reasonably accurate assessment of plaster walls, fireplaces, bathrooms, and perhaps additional floor space. Of these four factors, floor space is significant in both specifications, indicating that assessors seem to overvalue floor space by $1.40 to $1.60 per square foot. In addition, bathrooms are mildly significant in the first specifi-

---

[j]If there were a systematic relationship between the assessment *rate* and market value, this model would produce biased results. Evidence presented in the next chapter, page 96, suggests that assessment rate is independent of market value in the jurisdictions of concern here.

Table 4-8. Systematic Variation in Assessment Error: California

	Specification I β	Specification I t	Specification II β	Specification II t
Structural Characteristics				
Year Built (00–75)	13.3	1.3	−21.1	1.9
Construction Type (0–9, 9 = best)	667.6	3.1[b]	636.8	3.1[b]
Lot Size (1–5)	235.3	1.1	522.6	2.3[a]
Floor Space (sq. ft.)	−1.4	2.5[a]	−1.6	3.0[b]
Rooms (no.)	319.5	1.9	170.7	1.1
Quality (2–8, 8 = best)	891.0	3.9[b]	−188.2	0.8
Condition (1–9, 9 = best)	335.8	5.7[b]	150.0	2.4[a]
Bathrooms (× 10)	−82.4	2.3[a]	7.8	0.2
Air Conditioning (yes = 1)	−292.0	0.8	194.0	0.6
Swimming Pool (yes = 1)	−751.6	1.5	351.1	0.3
Garages (no.)	16.4	0.4	−17.6	0.5
Fireplace (no.)	−171.1	0.6	101.1	0.4
Plaster Walls (yes = 1)	150.7	0.1	−453.3	0.4
Finished Basement (yes = 1)	1066.4	1.1	290.6	0.3
Neighborhood Characteristics				
Access (20–135)	−12.3	1.7	—	—
Neighborhood Quality (2–9, 9 = best)	185.3	2.0[a]	—	—
Sewers (yes = 1)	2475	2.5[a]	—	—
Paved Roads (yes = 1)	410.8	0.2	—	—
Black Neighborhood (yes = 1)	786.5	1.0	—	—
Mexican Neighborhood (yes = 1)	1386	3.5[b]	—	—
Neighborhood 1	—	—	−1401	1.5
2	—	—	−394	0.5
3	—	—	−1015	1.2
4	—	—	−566	0.7
5	—	—	70	0.1
6	—	—	−245	0.3
7	—	—	3190	3.3[b]
8	—	—	3026	4.0[b]
9	—	—	3098	3.7[b]
10	—	—	3264	3.5[b]
11	—	—	2.6	0.0
12	—	—	1908	1.9[a]
13	—	—	−998	1.1
14	—	—	2670	3.5[b]
N	1014		1014	
R^2	.12		.21	

[a]Two-tailed t-test 5% critical value = 1.96.
[b]Two-tailed t-test 1% critical value = 2.57.

cation only. Plaster walls and fireplaces are insignificant in both specifications.

Among the remaining structural characteristics, both equations reveal evidence that assessors systematically undervalue the so-called better construction types. Since the type of construction is generally locked into a property for life and since tastes and construction technology change with time, the value of particular types of construction is likely to be dominated by positive and negative quasi-rents. In this case one would anticipate some error in an assessing system based on replacement costs.

The evidence in specification I suggests that assessors significantly undervalue quality and condition. However, there is colinearity evident between the quality and condition variables and the neighborhood dummies. When the fourteen dummies are added to the equation, quality turns from being highly significant ($t = 3.9$) to being totally insignificant ($t = 0.8$). In addition, condition turns from being highly significant ($t = 5.7$) to being mildly significant ($t = 2.4$). At the same time, the second specification indicates that properties located in neighborhoods seven through ten are undervalued by around $3,000 each. A likely explanation is that those neighborhoods are the better neighborhoods in town and that they contain the better quality houses in the best condition.[k] Those houses are clearly undervalued; the data are not sufficiently orthogonal to identify whether the assessor's error is based on quality and condition or whether the assessor has properly evaluated quality and condition but underestimated the location value of the neighborhood.

Two items of evidence point to systematic errors in the valuation of neighborhood characteristics. First, the introduction of exhaustive neighborhood dummies nearly doubles $\bar{R}^2$ (corrected) from .12 to .21. Second, five of the fourteen neighborhood dummy variables in specification II are highly significant and three of the six neighborhood characteristics in specification I are significant.

The partial Rs reported for the neighborhood characteristics in specification I indicate that they account for roughly 33 percent of the total explained variation in assessment error. Since the information added to the equation through the introduction of neighborhood dummies nearly doubles the amount of variation explained, it can be argued that inaccurate assessment of locational characteristics

---

[k]While it might be argued that the coefficients on the neighborhood dummy variables could result from the assessor's overestimating the "badness" of the less elegant neighborhoods, such an error would result in negative signs on the quality and condition variables rather than positive signs.

accounts for well over half and probably close to two-thirds of the 21 percent of observed assessment error that can be explained.

The data from the Boston SMSA contain less detail on neighborhood characteristics within jurisdictions and are thus less satisfactory for these purposes. On the other hand, by pooling those data across the fourteen jurisdictions, it should be possible to make a more general statement about common assessing errors associated with structural characteristics. The results of the estimation using the Massachusetts data are presented in Table 4-9.

While the data explain only 7 percent of the observed variation in assessment error, they tend to confirm the finding that the less malleable structural characteristics tend to be misassessed more consistently than the characteristics that can be easily altered. The most significant variables include lot size, year built, full basement, and fireplaces, all difficult or impossible to alter. Three of the four market-produced characteristics (modern kitchen, pool, and air conditioning) are insignificant as anticipated.

The significant dummy variables for one- and two-car garages were not anticipated. The sign on those variables indicates that assessors are overestimating the value of one- and particulary two-car garages. If contractors overbuilt houses with two-car garages, it is quite possible that negative quasi-rents have developed through time. That is, people are simply unwilling to pay the construction value for the additional garage. Since removal is impractical, implicit value falls below replacement cost, and assessors find themselves in error.

Brian Berry and Robert Bednarz in a recent article present evidence that seems to lend some support to the general conclusions of the analysis presented here[4]. They used data from a random sample of 275 single family homes in the city of Chicago that were sold during 1971. The data include information on five structural characteristics and eight neighborhood characteristics.

As part of their study, they regress the assessment-sales price ratio on structural and neighborhood characteristics. The characteristics that appear significant are number of interior square feet, age of the unit, the race of the neighborhood, and environmental quality. Once again this is suggestive that assessors err when estimating the value of neighborhood characteristics and nonmalleable structural characteristics.

To sum up the findings of this section, traditional assessing technology as described in commonly used assessing manuals does not differentiate between market-produced (malleable) structural characteristics and characteristics that are difficult to add or remove from a unit. The values of attributes that are less malleable often diverge

Table 4-9. Systematic Variation in Assessment Error: Massachusetts

	β	t
Structural Characteristics		
Brick Construction	-42.6	0.1
Modern Kitchen (1 = yes)	-148.5	0.4
Swimming Pool (1 = yes)	-1.09	0.0
Air Conditioning (1 = yes)	-71	0.0
Rooms (no.)	-140.0	1.4
Interior Space (sq. ft.)	.37	0.6
Baths (no.)	-1.0	0.0
One Car Garage (1 = yes)	-795.3	2.3[a]
Two-Car Garage (1 = yes)	-1867	4.5[b]
Full Basement (1 = yes)	-1383	2.4[a]
Construction Quality		
(1-9, 1 = best)	176.2	1.7[b]
Year Built (00-70)	-25.6	-3.3[b]
Fireplace (no.)	-605.0	-3.0[b]
Lot Size (sq. ft.)	-.04	5.8[b]
Neighborhood Characteristics		
Access (weighted distribution)	640.0	0.6
Percent Vacant Units (tract)	-26236	0.9
Median Income (tract)	.14	2.5[a]
Percent Low Status (tract)	-787.4	0.1
Percent Single Units (tract)	-149	0.1
Percent Black (tract)	35257	1.3
Population Density (tract)	.27	2.5[a]
N		2195
R^2		.07

[a]Two-tailed t-test 5% critical value = 1.96.
[b]Two-tailed t-test 1% critical value = 2.57.
Note: See Tables 4-6a, 4-6b, and 4-7 for a detailed description of each variable.

from replacement costs as locational quasi-rents arise. In addition, formal expositions of the traditional approach provide little guidance for the valuation of location-specific or neighborhood characteristics. The empirical evidence presented above reveals that while assessors' knowledge acquired through time may help correct these existing biases, they remain the source of considerable assessment error. Using the California data, it was shown that approximately 21 percent of assessment error was systematic and could be explained. The majority of the explained error seems to emerge from the inaccurate valuation of neighborhood characteristics. A large protion of the remainder seems to result from erroneous valuation of nonmalleable portions of the capital stock.

THE CAUSES OF VARIATION
WITHIN JURISDICTIONS:
SOME MACRO EVIDENCE

With the exception of the results found for the variation in towns with good performance, the analysis above employed data obtained from only two individual jurisdictions, Boston and Hanford, California. In order to further investigate the causes of variation in assessment performance, this section will employ aggregate data on a substantial number of jurisdictions within the Commonwealth of Massachusetts. Once again, the objective is to separate factors that cause variation in selling price and that are beyond the control of the local assessor from factors that can be affected by changes in assessment policy.

Even if a perfect assessment procedure was assumed, a significant amount of variation in assessment-sales ratios within jurisdictions would be observed. Sales do not all take place at a single time, and thus, no two sales take place under identical market conditions. More significant, however, is the fact that markets are imperfect. The first section of Chapter 3 discusses in some detail the concept of an equilibrium price distribution where buyers and sellers search with imperfect information.

The amount of variation in selling price within a jurisdiction should depend upon a number of factors. First, the institutional structure of the local real estate market should play a big role. In towns with an organized multiple listing service or where agents split fees and cooperate under informal agreements, buyers' information is likely to be inexpensive, and price distributions should have a relatively small variance because of more efficient search.

Second, since the most important data needed for property appraisal by buyers as well as assessors is exchange price information on previous sales, it is likely that jurisdictions with a higher volume of real estate transactions should have price distributions with smaller variance. This section will argue that towns with larger populations *ceteris paribus* are likely to have more total sales as well as a more integrated set of housing market institutions.

A third determinant of the amount of variation in sales price is the rate of change in the community. Jurisdictions that experience changes in housing demand or supply in a given period are likely to find a wider dispersion of housing prices as the market adjusts to the change.

The previous sections discussed specific problems with the generally accepted assessing technology. Given an existing and widely utilized technology, differences in assessing performance across jurisdictions holding sales price dispersions constant can arise from several sources. First is the frequency of reassessment. The previous section has demonstrated that significant increases in the coefficient of dispersion around the mean assessment-sales ratio take place through time when assessments do not change. Data compiled by a group at the Harvard Graduate School of Design for Concord, Massachusetts, reveal a trend toward wider variation in the years subsequent to Concord's 1969 revaluation[5].

A second source of cross-jurisdictional variation in assessing performance is the level of effort supplied by the town. If differences in technology and skill are ignored or controlled, one would assume that towns that devote a relatively high level of resources to the assessing process will perform better than towns that do not.

To test these hypotheses, the parameters of the following model were estimated using aggregate data on a substantial number of Massachusetts towns:

$$CD = \beta_0 + \beta_1 POP + \beta_2 \Delta POP + \beta_3 ADMINEXP \qquad (4\text{-}4)$$
$$+ \beta_4 REVAL$$

where

CD = Coefficient of dispersion around the mean assessment-sales ratio (1976 sales)

POP = 1970 population

ΔPOP = Percent change in population from 1960 to 1970

$ADMINEXP$ = Administrative expenditures for assessment and collection as a percentage of total tax collected

$REVAL$ = Number of years since the last full revaluation.

This relationship can be thought of as a production function for assessing services. Output, measured in quality units, is a function of inputs and environmental factors. Inputs are proxied here by expenditures on inputs and time since the last revaluation. This assumes implicitly that communities buy inputs at similar prices. Environmental factors are proxied by population and change in population. Production functions for public service outputs that have environmental factors as input were discussed by Bradford, Malt, and Oates in a 1969 essay[6].

Table 4-10. Coefficient of Dispersion of Assessment-Sales Ratios: Single Residential Properties by Deciles

Decile	Lower Limit	Upper Limit
Lowest	—	10.7
2nd	10.8	12.3
3rd	12.2	14.2
4th	14.3	16.2
5th	16.3	17.8
6th	17.9	19.4
7th	19.5	21.8
8th	21.9	26.3
9th	26.4	32.6
Highest	32.7	—

Source: Ibid., Table 10, p. 82.

The Data

In April 1977, the Department of Corporations and Taxation of the Commonwealth of Massachusetts published the first of a series of biennial reports on the tax bases in all of the over 300 towns and cities in the state. Based on a sample of 75,000 property sales statewide, a coefficient of dispersion was calculated for each of 270 towns from which a significant sample of sales was obtained.[1] The overall mean for the state is about 17.8. Roughly 10 percent of the 270 towns have coefficients below 10.7 percent and 10 percent have coefficients above 32.7 percent. Table 4-10 summarizes the data.

Information on administrative expenditures for assessment and collection purposes as well as total collections for each town were obtained from Massachusetts Bureau of Accounts in the Division of Corporations and Taxation. Cities and towns in the Commonwealth of Massachusetts are required by law to submit annually a Schedule A enumerating all receipts and expenditures by the local fisc broken down into minute categories. Prior to 1977, compliance was not universal. The data collected were for the calendar year 1972. In that year 195 towns submitted forms. Table 4-11 presents a sum-

---

[1]The coefficient was calculated as follows:

$$CD = \frac{\Sigma |A_i - \bar{A}|}{N \cdot \bar{A}}$$

where $\bar{A}$ = the mean assessment ratio for the jurisdiction, and N = the number of recorded sales. A_i = the ratio of assessed value to sales price for the i_{th} sale. See "1976 Equalized Valuations of Massachusetts Cities and Towns," Commonwealth of Massachusetts Department of Corporations and Taxation, April 1977, Table 10, p. 82.

Table 4-11. Administrative Expenditures for Assessment and Collection as a Percent of Property Tax Collected (calendar 1972)

Total Tax Collected (millions)	Number of Towns	Assess- ment[a] Group Mean	Collec- tion[b] Group Mean	Total Admin- istrative Costs	Assess- ment as Percent Total
0 - 0.2	15	1.14	.77	1.91	.59
0.2- 1.0	60	.73	.55	1.28	.57
1.0- 5.0	86	.71	.53	1.24	.57
5.0-10.0	23	.48	.39	.87	.55
>10.0	11	.38	.26	.64	.59
Overall	195	.70	.53	1.23	.56

[a]Includes normal annual expenditures for salaries of assessors and office force, salaries of maintaining block system, expenses for maintaining block system, printing, stationery, telephone and office expenses, auto rental. Excludes costs of major revaluations.

[b]Includes salaries of collector and office force, fees for special collectors, printing, stationery, telephone and office expenses, official bond, and advertising delinquent taxes.

Source: Unpublished *Schedules A* on file at the Commonwealth of Massachusetts, Division of Corporations and Taxation, Bureau of Accounts. Receipts, p. 1, line 1.1., and Payments, p. 12, lines 1.5. a and b. and 1.6.a and b.

mary of the information obtained. Administrative expenditures are split between collection and assessment functions. The data are grouped by size of total tax base.

It is interesting to note that the data suggest significant economies of scale in the production of both assessment and collection services. Total administrative costs decline from nearly 2 percent of total collections for smaller towns to less than two-thirds of 1 percent for the largest towns.

Census data on 144 towns within sixty minutes driving time of Boston (very roughly the eastern half of the state) were obtained from the *Universal Atlas of Eastern Massachusetts*[7].

To learn the year of the last major revaluation, a telephone survey of assessors was undertaken. Because of difficulties with telephone communications in general and doubts about the accuracy of information received, the survey was discontinued after twenty-six successful interviews.[m] While the model was estimated separately using this subsample of twenty-six towns, the full sample was run using a dummy variable for towns that had revalued since 1970

[m]Assessors were quite reluctant to give any information over the phone. Many stated, "We revalue each year."

instead of the number of years since revaluation. That more limited information was obtained from the state.

Table 4–12 presents summary statistics for the sample of seventy-nine towns for which all data were available:

Table 4–12.   Summary Statistics for Massachusetts Town Data, *N* = 79

Variable	Mean	Standard Deviation
CD	16.2	6.2
POP (000s)	16.8	13.5
ΔPOP (%)	42.2	50.1
ADMINEXP	0.55	0.19
REVAL (= 1 if since 1970 = 0 otherwise	0.19	0.39

The Results

Using the full sample of seventy-nine observations, the following results were obtained:

from the *Universal Atlas of Eastern Massachusetts*[7].

$$CD = 16.5 - 0.13\,POP - 0.003\Delta POP + 5.3ADMINEXP \quad (4\text{--}5)$$

$$ \underset{[2.5]}{(0.05)} \quad \underset{[0.2]}{(0.013)} \quad \underset{[1.44]}{(3.6)}$$

$$- 4.7\,REVAL$$
$$\underset{[3.0]}{(1.6)}$$

$$\bar{R}^2 = 0.24$$

Figures in parentheses are standard errors. Figures in brackets are *t*-statistics. The 1 percent critical value for a single-tailed *t*-test is 2.3.

The sign and magnitude of the coefficient on *POP* suggests that larger towns tend to have somewhat better performance. This may be because of a larger volume of transactions from which market actors obtain price data or because of the presence of a more integrated real estate market. While the coefficient on *POP* is significant at the 1 percent level, it is quite small. An increase in population of 15,000 (more than one standard deviation) will lower the coefficient of dispersion less than two points (less than one-third of one standard deviation).

The most significant variable is *REVAL*. The results indicate that towns that have revalued since 1970 have coefficients nearly five full points lower than towns that have not. This is consistent with previous evidence presented above.

Population change seems to have no observable effects on the coefficient of variation. It is possible that there may be two offsetting forces associated with a changing population. While a signficant amount of change will lead undoubtedly to changing patterns of attribute prices and land values, change also generates a larger volume of transactions.

The coefficient on *ADMINEXP* has the wrong sign and is mildly significant.[n] It was noted above that the tabulated data suggested the existence of economies of scale in both collection and assessment. While the presence of population as an independent variable will in part control for the size of the tax base, it is certainly an imperfect control. Since larger towns tend to perform better and larger towns spend less per dollar of collections on administration, it appears that towns that spend less perform better. To identify the effects of increased administrative expenditures, the function should be estimated using a stratified sample. The same relationship was estimated using the subsample of large jurisdictions (total base greater than $10 million). Within the smaller sample (thirteen), one town had not been revalued in twenty years while five were assessed in the seventies. In this estimation, two dummy variables were used, one for towns with recent revaluations and one for the town with the very old revaluation.

$$CD = 18.5 - 0.06\,POP + 0.05\,\Delta POP - 15.7\,ADMINEXP \quad (4\text{-}6)$$
$$ (0.036) \quad (0.028) \quad\quad (5.89)$$
$$ [1.65] \quad\; [1.72] \quad\quad\; [2.67]$$
$$ + \; 0.34\,NEW\,REVAL \quad + \quad 11.46\,OLD\,REVAL$$
$$ (0.68) \quad\quad\quad\quad\quad (1.6)$$
$$ [0.56] \quad\quad\quad\quad\quad [7.36]$$

$$\bar{R}^2 = 0.84$$

In this estimation, the coefficient on *ADMINEXP* is significant, has a negative sign, and is quite large.[o] The point estimate of that coefficient indicates that a 10 percent increase in expenditures lowers the coefficient of variation by 1.57 points.

[n]The *t*-statistic of 1.44 has a 2-tailed *P*-value of 0.14.

[o]The 5 percent critical value for a one-tailed *t*-test (7 d.f.) = 1.86.

A final estimation was accomplished using the full sample of towns where the actual date of revaluation was known. The $REVAL$ term in this equation is the number of years elapsed between the revaluation and 1976. There were a total of twenty-six such towns.

(4-7)

$$CD = 8.25 - 0.54\,POP - 0.012\,\Delta POP + 1.73\,ADMINEXP$$
$$(2.07)(0.034)\quad(0.017)\quad\quad(2.46)$$
$$[3.98][1.56]\quad\;[0.7]\quad\quad\;[0.7]$$

$$+\,0.82\,REVAL$$
$$(0.074)$$
$$[11.2]$$

$$\bar{R}^2 = 0.86$$

What emerges here is the great significance of the date of revaluation that dominates the equation. The simple correlation coefficient between $REVAL$ and CD is .93. The size of the coefficient on $REVAL$ is remarkably consistent with the results of the Harvard study of assessing in Concord, Massachusetts[8]. The coefficient here suggests that the coefficient of dispersion rises .82 points per year subsequent to revaluation. In Concord, the index rose from 10.0 to 16.6 between 1969 and 1973. From 1973 to 1974, it rose from 16.6 to 17.3.

CONCLUSIONS

Five significant conclusions emerge from this section: (1) larger jurisdictions, which are likely to have better integrated real estate markets and a larger volume of transactions, tend to have less variation in residential assessment rates than smaller communities; (2) assessment accuracy degenerates rapidly through time subsequent to major revaluation efforts; (3) the continuing level of administrative support exerted by assessing departments as measured by the level of expenditures does not seem to have a major effect on performance; (4) there seem to be significant economies of scale in assessing; and (5) the effects of environmental or community differences as measured by population and change in population are small relative to the effects of time lags in the assessment process.

These conclusions indicate that significant improvements in assessing performance even within the generally accepted assessing technology can be achieved through more frequent updating and revaluation. This further suggests that the single most important gain from switching to a multiple regression system of assessing is the ease with which current data on sales can be used to update existing assessments.

Chapter 5

The Implications of Effective Rate Variation Within Jurisdictions: Tax Capitalization

This chapter will explore some specific economic implications of rate variations within jurisdictions. The focus will be on the issue of tax capitalization and tax incidence.

Economicsts have been arguing about the incidence of the property tax since the days of Ricardo. A reading of the contemporary literature reveals no consensus and a good deal of confusion[1]. This should not be surprising given the complexity of the tax. The rate of taxation differs from jurisdiction to jurisdiction and region to region. Within jurisdictions effective rates have been shown to vary extensively. The final incidence of the tax depends upon factor supply responses and resource movements that occur as a result of the differentials.

Recent criticism of the tax reform literature points out that most analysts proceed as if they were designing an optimal taxation system *de novo*[2]. Reform measures are, of course, introduced into a world where resource flows and asset values have adjusted to the pre-reform tax structure. This portion of Chapter 5 will argue that the issue of tax capitalization is of particular import to those concerned with the property tax. The section begins with a discussion of how site or location values are likely to have adjusted to both inter- and intra-jurisdictional differentials in effective rates of taxation. The section concludes with empirical tests of the capitalization hypotheses utilizing the two large micro data bases discussed in Chapter 4, pages 33 to 70. It will be argued that previous attempts to empirically capture such effects have erred in a variety of ways.

THE THEORY OF TAX CAPITALIZATION

Since the bulk of the incidence literature is set in the context of the competitive market model, this analysis will begin with the competitive case and the traditional assumptions. The assumptions of perfectly mobile capital and labor, or (equivalently) the assumption of long-run equilibrium, will be relaxed later.

In such a model, land will be used by those who submit the highest bid for it. The value of an individual bid is determined by the amount of excess profit the user would earn on reproducible capital if the location or lot were free.

If we assume perfect information and perfect capital markets, landowners would be able to extract from users the full amount of any expected surplus over and above a normal rate of return (including considerations of risk) on the reproducible mobile capital after depreciation. In some instances the return to land and capital may be in the form of an explicit rental or profit stream. In others, where ownership and use are coincident, returns may be in a nonpecuniary form. The return to location and structure that is earned by homeowners has come to be called imputed rent.

The bids offered for particular locations derive from the characteristics of the location. Commercial or industrial bidders may find transportation cost savings or access to a large retail market result in a higher return on investment. Those bidding for residential location (owners or landlords) are purchasing accessibility, good (or bad) schools, other sundry neighborhood amenities, and a tax rate. This section examines how bids are likely to respond to tax rate differentials.

Traditional analysis of property tax incidence begins with a distinction between the portion of the tax that is on land and the portion that is on improvements or capital[3]. Most property taxes are ideally a uniform tax on the total asset value of a property. A property administered tax would rise whenever site values (land rents) rise or when the capital component of the property is increased.

It is noramlly held that the portion of the tax falling on the land component of the asset package is fully borne by the landowner and that imposition of the tax causes the price of land to fall by the capitalized value of the tax[4]. Feldstein has shown that even this assertion is not correct since shifting can take place in a number of ways[5].

First, there may be income effects if landowners earn other forms of income; supplies of other factors may respond to the decline in rental income. Second, the decline in asset value overall may stimulate savings and, hence, capital accumulation. Finally, the change in land values may cause a portfolio imbalance that slightly increases the demand for land and leads to somewhat less than full capitalization of the tax. While these effects are not likely to be large, there is at least some reason to expect less than full capitalization of even the land component.

The bulk of the tax incidence literature focuses on the portion of the tax that falls on improvements. If the tax were a well-administered uniform national tax on all capital assets, shifting would only occur if the supply of capital adjusted to the lower post-tax rate of return. Without such a response, the full burden of the tax would be borne by capital income earners.

However, the property tax is not a national tax; it is primarily a local tax that is generally poorly administered. As such, differential rates cause interindustry and interjurisdictional resource flows that shift the tax in a variety of directions. While the analysis of such shifts is not difficult in the context of a two-sector model like that of Harberger, the property tax is more complicated[6]. There are five types of capital flow that should be explicitly considered: (1) flows into and out of metropolitan areas; (2) flows into and out of jurisdictions within metropolitan areas; (3) flows between housing submarkets; (4) flows between export producing industries and local goods producing industries (including housing); and (5) flows within jurisdictions between neighborhoods.

If we begin with a set of jurisdictions at equilibrium with uniform taxation and then raise the tax on improvements in *one* jurisdiction on *one* type of industry (or one type of housing), such an increase lowers the rate of return to that capital.[a] In the current model, the capitalist responds in two ways. First, since a higher rate of return can be earned in other sectors or locations, capital flows from the now higher tax jurisdiction (sector) to the lower tax jurisdictions (sectors); rates of return and prices adjust appropriately. Second, land rent bids in the taxed jurisdiction fall.

Where the jurisdiction or sector with the higher tax rate is small relative to the rest of the world, capital simply flows out until the post-tax return rises to the pretax level, which is exogenously determined in the capital market.

From the point of view of an individual firm, the price of capital is higher after the tax. To increase its capital stock by one unit, the firm must pay for the capital plus a higher tax on the now larger stock. To the extent that factors are substitutable, the optimal

[a]Note that we assume the tax is not spent locally. It can be argued that this is an inappropriate way to view local tax incidence since taxes and expenditures are linked and both affect the real return on investment.

capital stock is altered. At the new equilibrium, the land rent bid must necessarily be lower. Thus, a portion of the tax on improvements is clearly passed on to landowners and capitalized in the form of lower land or location values.

To illustrate these points, consider a simple model with a Cobb-Douglas technology. Suppose that housing is produced using only capital and land and that the housing market is competitive. Assume that individual producers use the following technology:

$$Q = AK^\alpha L^\beta \tag{5-1}$$

where

Q = Quantity of housing services
K = Quantity of capital inputs
L = Quantity of land inputs.

As long as capital markets are competitive, landowners should be able to extract

$$RL = P(AK^\alpha L^\beta) - rK \tag{5-2}$$

where

P = Equilibrium price of housing services
r = Market price of capital inputs
R = Bid rent per unit of land

Furthermore, competition will force producers to maximize R. If we assume that lot size is predetermined, we can focus on the investment decision of individual producers.

Maximizing Equation 5-2 with respect to K, we obtain

$$K^* = \left(\frac{r}{\alpha PAL^\beta} \right)^{\frac{1}{\alpha-1}} \tag{5-3}$$

an expression for the optimal capital stock. Differentiating Equation 5-3 with respect to r yields

$$\frac{\partial K^*}{\partial r} = \frac{1}{\alpha-1} \left(\alpha PAL^\beta \right)^{\frac{1}{1-\alpha}} r^{\frac{2-\alpha}{\alpha-1}} \tag{5-4}$$

Multiplying by $r*/K$ we obtain an expression for the elasticity of K with respect to r:

$$\frac{dK*}{dr} \cdot \frac{r}{K*} = \frac{1}{\alpha-1} \qquad (5\text{-}5)$$

Thus if the increased property tax raises the price of capital, r, to the firm, capital will flow out. In a Cobb-Douglas world the rate depends only on capital's share of total product.[b] In a more general formulation, the amount of outflow depends on the elasticity of substitution in the taxed jurisdiction. Note that a large capital share implies a fairly large capital elasticity in the case where the elasticity of substitution is unity. If $\alpha = .75$, for example, the elasticity of K with respect to r is equal to -4.

To determine the impact of such changes in the firm's bid for land we substitute Equation 5-3 into Equation 5-2 and divide by L:

$$R = \left[PA \left(\alpha PAL^\beta \right)^{\frac{\alpha}{1-\alpha}} L^{\beta-1} - \left(\alpha PAL^\beta \right)^{\frac{1}{1-\beta}} L^{-1} \right] r^{\frac{\alpha}{\alpha-1}} \quad (5\text{-}6)$$

Equation 5-6 is an expression for the bid rent offered per unit of land by the firm. To obtain an expression for the responsiveness of bid rents with respect to tax differentials, we differentiate Equation 5-6 with respect to r and multiply by r/R. This yields:

$$\frac{dR}{dr} \cdot \frac{r}{R} = \frac{\alpha}{1-\alpha} \qquad (5\text{-}7)$$

since $0 < \alpha < 1$, $\alpha/\alpha - 1 < 0$. Here again, the responsiveness depends only upon capital's share of total output. Where capital's share is large, bid rents fall quickly in response to tax-induced changes in r. If, for example, $\alpha = 0.75$, the elasticity of R with respect to r is -3. In the more general case, the responsiveness of rents will depend, in addition, on the elasticity of substitution in the taxed sector. In the limit, if the elasticity of substitution were zero, no capital would flow out and rents would fall by the full amount of the tax.

The purpose of this exercise has been to demonstrate that even in the case where capital stocks adjust fully and where substantial factor substitutability is possible, landowners bear a significant portion of a differential property tax on improvements. In reality, housing capital adjusts slowly and there is probably less substitutability than

[b]This assumes homogeneity or $\alpha + \beta = 1$.

a Cobb-Douglas technology implies[7]. Relaxation of the mobile capital assumption or assuming a lower elasticity of substitution both imply that land will bear *more* of the tax. Thus, the degree of shifting on to land implied in the above exercise can be thought of as a lower bound. Where rates differ within jurisdictions among classifications (i.e., commercial, industrial, and residential) and where differentials are expected to persist, the analysis is precisely the same as above. Each sector would adjust independently to the exogenously determined price of capital. Where differentials are large, they could have an effect on the outcome of the bidding process. That is, housing producers might offer higher bids for a piece of land that would have been used for a commercial establishment in the absence of tax differentials among property types.[c]

Similarly, to the extent that tax rate differentials within jurisdictions are neighborhood specific and expected to persist, one might observe capital flows between neighborhoods. Again the above analysis is appropriate.

Thus far we have assumed a well-administered correct tax—that is, a tax that is imposed onto true value of land and improvements that adjust instantaneously to changes in that value. Chapter 2 has demonstrated, however, that the property tax is not a well-administered tax. Tax bases are generally adjusted infrequently and there exists a good deal of effective rate variation within jurisdictions.

Here the analysis differs. If investments or disinvestments do not affect the assessment of the property and if reassessment is unanticipated at any time in the future, the price of capital does not reflect the tax at the margin, and the optimal capital stock is unaffected. Such a tax is equivalent to a lump sum tax since marginal decisions are unaffected. As a result, differentials that arise are fully capitalized into land prices.

Where intrajurisdictional tax differentials occur as the result of simple assessment error or as a result of changes in parcel values through time, the extent to capitalization and, hence, the final incidence of the tax depends upon the character and frequency of reassessment as well as the appeal or abatement procedures in effect. If, for example, properties were reassessed upon sale, one would expect to find no capitalization of differentials within jurisdictions and within property classifications. Similarly, if reassessment takes place only on appeal, one might expect to find asymmetric capitalization. That is, underassessed properties sell for more than they would if

[c]Such a scenario is not likely because of the widespread use of land use controls, which tend to be inflexible. Only where bid differentials were large would one expect to find zoning changes enacted.

properly assessed, but overassessed properties would not sell for less.

As Feldstein points out, tax capitalization presents policymakers with something of a dilemma[8]. Consider the case of a single under-assessed house. Presumably, when the house is sold in the market the exchange price will be higher than the price of an identical properly assessed house by the present value of the unanticipated tax savings that will accrue to the buyer. The seller of the unit absconds with the entire savings. If the assessment is corrected at a later date, the buyers have not only lost their tax savings but the unit depreciates by the present value of that loss. Hence, the owner at the time of reform pays the additional tax twice.[d]

Feldstein argues that such inequities could be corrected if a proper compensation scheme were to accompany the institution of reform[9]. At the same time he is careful to present a variety of arguments for denying or reducing compensation.

EMPIRICAL EVIDENCE OF TAX CAPITALIZATION

The capitalization of differentials in effective rates of property taxation has been examined empirically by a number of authors. The emphasis of this literature, however, has been on cross-jurisdictional differences in tax rates. The earliest empirical works were done by Jensen (1931) and Daicoff (1961)[10]. However, two more recent pieces by Orr (1968) and Oates (1969) have sparked considerable interest and discussion in the literature[11].

Oates uses aggregate data on fifty-three municipalities in New Jersey to estimate the parameters of a simple hedonic price index.

$$V = 29 - 3.6 \text{ LOG } T + 4.9 \text{ LOG } E - 1.3 \text{ LOG } M \qquad (5\text{-}8)$$
$$(2.3)(3.2) \qquad\qquad (2.1) \qquad\qquad (4.0)$$
$$+ 1.6\,R + 0.06\,N + 1.5\,Y + 0.3\,P$$
$$(3.6) \quad (3.9) \quad (7.7) \quad (3.1)$$

where

V = Median value of single family homes in thousands

T = Average effective tax rate 1956–1960

E = Current expenditures per pupil

---

[d]Note that there would be no inequity if the reform were fully anticipated at the time of sale.

R = Median number of rooms per owner-occupied unit
N = Percent of houses built since 1950
Y = Median family income
P = Percent of families with less than $1,000 in income
M = Linear distance to downtown Manhattan.

Since E and T are simultaneously determined with V, Oates employs a two-stage procedure using a number of additional exogenous variables to identify T and E, among them the percentage of population in elementary school and the percentage of the housing stock that is owner occupied.

The positive and significant coefficient on the tax variable Oates interprets as strong evidence of tax capitalization. He states, "The size of the coefficients suggests that, for an increase in property taxes unaccompanied by an increase in local public services, the bulk of the rise in taxes will be capitalized in the form of reduced property values"[12].

There has been substantial literature criticizing the Oates model on a variety of grounds. For the purpose of this section the most important are the writings that are ciritical of the econometric specification and data[13].

George Meadows uses the same data set but formulates a complete four-equation model[14]. His dependent variables are median value of owner-occupied housing, the equalized property tax rate, school expenditures per pupil and per capita municipal expenditures. While the more explicit simultaneous equation formulation is pleasing, the independent variables are a collection of municipal average characteristics that are divided up among the four equations in a haphazard manner. There is no compelling reason, for example, why population density is likely to affect municipal expenditures per resident and not school expenditures or property values directly.

A. Thomas King argues in a recent article that Oates and others who have attempted empirically to capture the effects of the tax differentials on property values have used an erroneous specification of the tax variable, which leads to an upward bias of the estimated capitalization effect[15]. King points out that Oates's estimated effect of a change in the tax rate on the value of single family housing is "independent of the value of the dwelling[16]. The proper term, he argues, is a "tax payment" term that reflects the actual increase in taxes resulting from a change in rate. King's results indicate that the original Oates estimate of capitalization is about 40 percent too great; yet he is content to cautiously conclude, "I believe our knowledge of the extent of tax capitalization is very much less than is commonly supposed"[17].

Again using Oates's data, Rosen and Fullerton compound matters further by arguing that Oates's use of input rather than output data for public service levels results in a downward bias in the estimate of the capitalization rate[18]. By switching from per pupil expenditure to a set of test scores, we find "the [tax] capitalization ratio increases considerably"[19].

Orr's approach to the problem of tax capitalization is somewhat different[20]. By focusing on rental housing and including land value as an independent variable, Orr claims to test for the capitalization of the improvement portion of the tax only. Using aggregate data on thirty-one Boston communities, Orr finds no significant relationship between rent level and tax rates and concludes that a "substantial portion" of property taxes on the improvement component of urban rental housing is borne by property owners[21].

In a critique of Orr's work, Heinberg and Oates use Orr's data to estimate the parameters of a model similar to Oates' earlier model discussed above[22]. Again using median value of owner-occupied housing as a dependent variable in a simple hedonic index estimation, they conclude that "differentials in local property tax rates on owner occupied housing are capitalized"[23].

The most significant problem with all these studies is the very real possibility of significant omitted variable bias resulting from their use of aggregate data. All utilize a relatively small set of community descriptors available from the census. Certainly intercommunity differences in the type (quality) of housing stocks is not well captured by the one or two variables included in most of the studies. In addition, the discussion of Chapter 3 indicates a substantial number of neighborhood characteristics that micro studies have found significant in determining housing and land values. When such variables are omitted, their effects can be attributed to related variables that are included.

The omission of crime rates is a case in point. Obviously, a high crime rate reduces the attractiveness of a community and is likely to result in lower property values. At the same time, more crime may necessitate increased expenditure on police and fire and thus a higher tax rate. Similar effects may result if the probability of fire is improperly controlled for.

Since the inclusion of more variables leads quickly to problems of multicolinearity when aggregate data are utilized, these difficulties can be overcome only through the use of micro data. While the use of detailed data on individual transactions enables analysts to control for the characteristics of the unit, it has the added feature of allowing them to test for the capitalization of intrajurisdictional tax differences.

While a number of major studies have employed micro data to estimate the parameters of hedonic price indexes, the issue of tax capitalization has been secondary or even incidental in most[24]. Two studies, however, have directly addressed the issue.

The first, a 1973 study by A. Thomas King, utilizes a sample of 1,892 single family homes located in and around New Haven, Conneticut, that were sold between 1967 and 1969[25]. King uses ordinary least squares to estimate the parameters of the following model:

$$\text{Price} = \sum_{i=1}^{m} \alpha_i SC_i + \sum_{j=1}^{n} \beta_j LC_j + \gamma(D)L \qquad (5\text{-}9)$$

where

SC_i is the ith structural characteristic
LC_j is the jth location characteristic
L is the quantity of land purchased and
$\gamma(D)$ the price per unit, a function of
the accessibility of the location to
the CBD.

The data contain information on twenty-three structural characteristics and eleven neighborhood or location characteristics.

King claims to test for the capitalization of interjurisdictional differences only; yet his tax term is specified in such a way as to capture differences both within and among jurisdictions. He states:

Two kinds of tax differentials exist: the legal differences between towns and the illegal differences within towns. Theories of tax capitalization have considered only the first of these. But illegal differences are as prevalent and as large as legal differences, and since illegal differences themselves are unlikely to be capitalized and furthermore tend to prevent capitalization of legal differences because of the confusion they create, the probability of observing tax capitalization is not so great as the simple calculation of legal tax differentials would imply[26].

The theory presented at the beginning of this section suggests that both intrajurisdictional and interjurisdictional tax differentials are likely to be capitalized if assessments are not frequently revised. It will be argued below that purchasers are likely to consider the tax rate and the actual assessment separately and proper specification would include two tax-savings variables.

King constructs his single term as follows:

$$TAXDIF = r_a \cdot AV - r_L \cdot AV \qquad\qquad (5\text{-}10)$$

where

r_a = Mill rate in town where the property
  is located
r_L = Mill rate in the low tax reference town
AV = Assessed value of the property.

There are a number of serious problems with such a specification. First, it eliminates the most important single source of interjuris-dictional variation, differences in assessment procedures and rates of assessment. Second, inclusion of assessed value in this fashion creates an identification problem for the equation. Assessed value and market value should be strongly related in a positive way since both are a function of the included right-hand variables. Capitalization of intrajurisdictional differentials would lead to a negative relation-ship between AV and market value. Since all of these effects are likely to have an impact on the estimated coefficient on $TAXDIF$, it is not surprising that it turns out to be insignificantly different from zero.

What is surprising is King's explanation for that finding: "the assessed value of property for tax purposes is such an irregular proportion of market value that buyers may be unable to discern differentials which result from statutory tax rates or to separate them from differentials which reflect poor or obsolete assessments[27]. The empirical results of King's study are insufficient to reject the null hypotheses of no capitalization[28].

The only empirical study to focus explicitly on tax rate differen-tials within taxing jurisdictions was done by Church in 1974[29]. Church uses a set of 957 observations on single family homes sold in Martinez, California, from 1968 through 1970. While his model is substantially more complicated, it offers a more reasonable specifica-tion of the intrajurisdictional effect.

He begins by assuming that

$$P = \sum_{i=1}^{T} \frac{(Y_i - t_i P)}{(1 + r)^i}$$

where

$$P = \text{Market value of the house}$$
$$t_i = t_i^\gamma \ (A/P) \quad A = \text{Assessed value of the unit,}$$
$$t_i^\gamma = \text{Nominal tax rate in year } i.$$
$$r = \text{Appropriate discount rate}$$
$$Y = \text{Pretax net annual rent.}$$

If we allow

$$K = \sum_{i=1}^{T} \frac{1}{(1+r)^i}, \tag{5-12}$$

then

$$P = \frac{K \cdot Y}{1 + Kt} \tag{5-13}$$

or

$$P = \frac{K \cdot Y}{(1 + Kt)^b} \tag{5-14}$$

where b indicates the extent of tax capitalization.

If V is the unobservable fair market rent in the absence of the tax, then $V = KY$. Church assumes that

$$V = \prod_{j=1}^{N} X_j{}^{a_j} \tag{5-15}$$

where the Xs are property characteristics.

Substituting Equation (5-15) into Equation (5-14) for the unobservable $V = KY$ and taking logs, Church obtains his primary equation:

$$\text{LOG } P = \sum_{j=1}^{N} (a_j \text{LOG } X_j) - b \text{ LOG } (1 + Kt) \tag{5-16}$$

a double log hedonic price index with a fairly simple tax capitalization term. Recall that since $T = t^\gamma(A/P)$ the variation in the far right-hand term comes from the assessment-sales ratio.

Church's second simultaneous equation is somewhat less satisfactory. He assumes that the effective tax rate is a linear function of P. That is,

$$t = c + dP \qquad (5\text{-}17)$$

There is no justification for the existence of such a relationship offered, and while it is not entirely unreasonable, a less rigid specification is preferable and will be discussed below. It is not clear how such a linear restriction is likely to affect the estimate of b.

In estimating the parameters of the model, Church uses principle component analysis to reduce a set of ninety independent variables to a manageable set of orthogonal characteristics. The sample is segmented by neighborhood and the estimates of b are large and significant in each subsample, indicating overcapitalization.

Although overcapitalization is difficult to explain theoretically, Church presents a few unconvincing scenarios including the capitalization of the deadweight loss from the tax.[e]

AN EMPIRICAL ANALYSIS OF TAX CAPITALIZATION

The analysis presented here uses the large micro data bases discussed in Chapter 4 to test for the existence of tax capitalization. In addition to searching for further evidence of the capitalization of interjurisdictional differences, the analysis separately tests for evidence of the capitalization of two types of intrajurisdictional tax differentials: (1) systematic variation in tax rates by neighborhood and (2) differences between units not related to location, that is, random over- and underassessment. Previous studies have failed to make the latter important distinction.

Testing for the capitalization of neighborhood differentials is conceputally no different from testing for cross-jurisdictional capitali-

---

[e]In many California towns, nominal tax rates vary significantly from neighborhood to neighborhood depending on the elementary school district and upon provision of water, sewer, and garbage pickup services. While a single town was chosen to control for public service levels, it is quite possible that such variation exists within the town. If it does, and I have no evidence to that effect specific to Martinez, it would account for the observer "overcapitalization." In Hanford, California, a similar town, there are thirteen separate nominal rates listed in the rate catalogue.

zation. Estimations looking for the capitalization of more random assessment errors, on the other hand, are plagued by serious biases that would preclude the identification of such effects even if they existed. Such biases have not previously been discussed in the literature.

The Data

Two data sets were utilized in the empirical work to follow. The first contains observations on 2,195 single family homes, located in thirteen predominantly white suburban Boston communities, that were sold in 1971. For each sale the data contain information on seventeen structural characteristics and ten neighborhood descriptions along with assessed value and selling price.

The second contains observations on 1,084 single family units sold between 1972 and 1975 in Hanford, California. These data contain information on eighteen structural characteristics and five neighborhood attributes. For a detailed descriptions of both data sets, see Chapter 4, Empirical Evidence of Tax Capitalization.

Interjurisdictional Differences

Using the Boston data, the parameters of a liner hedonic price index were estimated:

$$V = \beta_0 + \sum_{i=1}^{N} \beta_i X_i + \gamma T \tag{5-18}$$

where

V = Sales price of the unit
x_i = Unit characteristic i
T = Term reflecting the variation in taxation across cities.

Two specifications were employed in the estimations. In the first model, the equalized tax rate was included without adjustment. As King points out, inclusion of a term like this tends to overstate the amount of capitalization on lower value units and understate the amount of capitalization on higher value units[30]. This is so because the linear model constrains the estimated effect of a one-mill change in the tax rate to be a constant dollar amount regardless of the house value range.

To be responsive to King's criticism, a second model was estimated in which the equalized tax rate was multiplied by the predicted sales price of the unit from a first-state regression of price on the characteristics. Since the fitting values of "*P*" contain only information already contained in the included characteristics, it serves as a scaling factor without introducing any unwanted variation into the tax term. In model II,

$$T = M \cdot \overline{AR} \cdot \hat{SP} \qquad (5\text{-}19)$$

where

M = Nominal tax rate
$\overline{AR}$ = Mean assessment-sales ratio for the jurisdiction
$\hat{SP}$ = Predicted sales price of the unit
$\hat{SP}$ = $\hat{\beta}_0 + \Sigma \hat{\beta}_i X_i$

X_i = Structural or neighborhood characteristic *i*.

It might be argued that T should be specified as the difference between the actual tax bill and the tax bill if the unit were located in the lowest tax jurisdiction in the sample, Since the only variation in T as specified in both models comes from rate variation, the equation is already implicitly making such a comparison.

The results of the estimations are presented in Table 5-1 and reveal convincing evidence of significant tax capitalization across jurisdictions. The equations contain fourteen and fifteen variables, respectively, significant of the 1 percent level in two-tailed tests. Signs and magnitudes of all significant coefficients are reasonable.

The coefficient on the tax rate in model I suggests that a rise in taxes of $1 per thousand dollars of assessed valuation lowers unit value by $214. Such a figure would represent full capitalization of a one-mill rate increase on a $20,000 home if the differential were capitalized at 7 percent for twenty years. For higher income houses, such a figure suggests undercapitalization.

The coefficient on the tax bill in model II suggests that a $1 rise in tax bill results in an $8.82 decrease in house value. Full capitalization of such a change at a discount rate of 7 percent for thirty years would result in a $13 change in value. Employing a higher discount rate to account for risk, such a figure is probably very close to what the full capitalization hypothesis would suggest.

Table 5-1. Interjurisdictional Tax Capitalization: Boston Suburban Data
$N = 2195$

	Model I		Model II	
	β	t	β	t
Constant	*24,760*	*7.6*	*22,600*	*7.8*
Lot Size	.22	25.7	.31	18.0
Floor Space	6.6	9.8	8.6	11.6
Quality	-1,649	13.3	-2,260	15.1
Rooms	-110	0.9	-101	0.8
Year Built	78	8.6	107	10.4
Baths	635	19.1	866	17.6
Fireplace (no.)	1,007	4.2	1,355	5.5
Modern Kitchen (D)	311	0.9	406	1.1
Full Basement (D)	-1,027	1.5	-1,519	2.2
Brick or Stone (D)	1,239	1.6	1,524	2.0
One-Car Garage (D)	649	1.6	902	2.2
Two-Car Garage (D)	2,752	5.6	3,747	7.2
>Two-Car Garage	6,006	3.3	8,049	4.4
Central Air	2,266	1.3	3,016	1.7
Swim Pool	5,691	3.4	7,915	4.7
Access	-3,628	2.9	-5,470	4.7
Income (tract)	.34	4.9	.50	6.6
Vacant Units (tract)	-44,109	1.2	-56,968	1.6
Low Status (tract)	-14,923	2.2	-19,050	2.8
Density	.56	4.5	.69	5.6
Per Pupil Expenditures	2.12	1.1	2.4	1.3
Tax Rate[a]	-214	4.0	—	—
Tax Bill[b]	—	—	-8.82	6.4
$\bar{R}^2$		.82		.82

[a]Equalized tax rate = nominal rate · (mean assessment ratio).
[b]Equalized tax rate · (predicted unit value) or tax rate · $\hat{P}$ where $\hat{P} = \sum_i \hat{\gamma}_1 X_1$ from first stage

Note: two tailed t-test, critical value $\left. \begin{matrix} 1\% = 2.57 \\ 5\% = 1.96. \end{matrix} \right\}$

In summary, the data reveal a significant amount of evidence in support of the capitalization hypothesis.

Intrajurisdictional Differentials

Conceptually, tax differentials that arise within jurisdiction but which are neighborhood specific are no different from interjurisdictional differences. It is as if separate assessors were taxing each neighborhood.

Because of the substantial number of neighborhoods identified, the California data are ideally suited for examining such neighborhood specific variations. These data were used to estimate the parameters of two models identical to those presented above. That is,

$$V = \beta_0 + \sum_i \beta_i X_i + \gamma T \qquad (5\text{-}20)$$

where

T = Mean assessment-sales ratio for the neighborhood containing the observation in model I

$T = M \cdot \overline{AR} \cdot \hat{P}$ in model II

and

M = Local nominal tax rate (.01208)

$\overline{AR}$ = Mean assessment-sales ratio for the neighborhood of the observation

$\hat{P}$ = Fitted values of a first-stage regression of sales price on the unit characteristics including the tax term.

The parameter estimates are presented in Table 5-2. There are twelve coefficients significant at the 1 percent level. Overall, the equations explain about 83 percent of the variation in market price. Significant variables all have the predicted signs and reasonable magnitudes.

While the coefficients on the tax terms are suggestive of capitalization, they must be interpreted with caution. First, while they have the correct signs and reasonable magnitudes, they are only mildly significant. Second, in the regressions above using the Boston data, there was a good deal of detailed information on neighborhood characteristics included in the model. Here, since all observations are drawn from one jurisdiction, the model relies primarily on a crudely constructed quality index, access, and dummies for black and Mexican neighborhoods. It is possible that unobserved and omitted neighborhood characteristics systematically related to the assessment-sales ratio produced the observed effects.

Consider, for example, if expectations concerning the future of a neighborhood resulted in a depressed average selling price during the sample period. The mean assessment ratio (*AV/SP*) would appear

Table 5-2. Capitalization of Intrajurisdiction Variation by Neighborhood: California Data, N = 1014

	Model I		Model II	
	β	t	β	t
Constant	-19,620	6.1	-26,320	8.9
Lot Size (1-5)	1,787	7.2	2,161	7.8
Floor Space (sq. ft.)	10.3	16.0	12.2	14.9
Rooms (no.)	-163	0.8	-212	1.1
Quality (2-8, 8 = best)	2,174	8.3	2,564	8.9
Year Built (00-75)	120	10.1	141	11.1
Baths (no.)	158	3.8	183	4.4
Fireplaces (no.)	2,066	6.6	2,431	7.3
Garages (no.)	18.5	0.4	21.7	0.5
Condition (1-9, 9 = best)	298	4.2	362	4.9
Construction (0-9, 9 = best)	-506	2.0	-593	2.4
Exterior Condition (0-3, 3 = best)	-495	1.2	-565	1.4
Heating (0-5, 0 = best)	-117	1.1	-143	1.3
Basement (yes = 1)	1,754	1.6	2,340	2.1
Swimming Pool (yes = 1)	4,162	7.5	4,890	8.3
Air Conditioning (yes = 1)	1,123	2.9	1,332	3.5
Sewer Tie-in (yes = 1)	1,643	1.4	1,851	1.6
Paved Road (yes = 1)	5,081	2.2	5,842	2.5
In Black Neighborhood (yes = 1)	-2,958	3.2	-3,876	4.1
In Mexican Neighborhood (yes = 1)	-1,151	2.5	-1,485	3.1
Access (20-135)	-8.5	0.9	-6.9	0.8
NBHD Condition (2-9, 9 = best)	175	1.5	149	1.3
Neighborhood Tax Rate[a]	-3,426	-2.2	—	—
Neighborhood Tax Bill[b]	—	—	-16.6	3.4
$\bar{R}^2$		.83		.83

[a]Mean assessment sales ratio in the neighborhood of the observation.
[b]$A\bar{R} \cdot M \cdot P$ see text for description.
Note: two tailed t-test, critical value $\left\}\begin{array}{l} 1\% = 2.57 \\ 5\% = 1.96. \end{array}\right.$

larger than the community average, and sales prices would be lower than predicted. Such an effect would result in a negative coefficient on the tax term; that is also what capitalization would predict.

The point estimate of γ in model II, if interpreted as the tax capitalization effect, suggests at least full capitalization. A $1 increase in tax bill would result in a $16 decrease in unit price. While these results must be cautiously interpreted, they do suggest that some significant capitalization of neighborhood tax differentials may be taking place.

Random Differentials Within Jurisdictions

Testing for capitalization of random assessment error within jurisdictions presents some different and difficult problems.

In testing for capitalization of such differentials, one would like to estimate the parameters of a model of the following form:

$$SP = \beta_0 + \sum_i \beta_i X_i + \gamma T + \lambda m (AV' - AV) + e \qquad (5\text{-}21)$$

$$AV = b_0 + \sum_i b_i X_i + u \qquad (5\text{-}22)$$

where

$$
\begin{aligned}
x_i &= \text{Housing unit characteristic } i \\
T &= \text{Measure of the local or neighborhood} \\
&\quad\text{effective tax rate for this type of unit} \\
m &= \text{Nominal tax rate} \\
AV' &= \text{Proper assessed value of the unit} \\
AV &= \text{Actual assessed value of the unit} \\
SP &= \text{Selling price of the unit.}
\end{aligned}
$$

If T is properly specified, it will indicate the rate of capitalization of interjurisdictional or interneighborhood rate differentials. $m(AV' - AV)$ is a term that reflects the annual dollar savings to the homeowner resulting from random underassessment or dollar loss resulting from random overassessment.

If the model were to be estimated using data from a single jurisdiction, T would be dropped along with the Xs specific to the taxing jurisdiction and uniform across the city.

Three major problems plague attempts to estimate such a model: (1) unobservable or omitted variables, (2) simultaneity, and (3) randomness in market price formation. While the discussion below will focus on property tax capitalization, these difficulties bear on the empirical examinations of tax capitalization in general.

Both assessed and market value are hypothesized to be functions of the characteristics of the unit. If the set of X's was exhaustive and the errors independent, the model would be fully recursive and would satisfy the assumptions required for *OLS* estimation. While many data sets are complete, there are always unobservables that can be detected by both assessors and buyers. If, for example, two houses, *A* and *B*, were identical in every way except that *A* was built in a style that was currently in vogue, buyers would be likely to bid more for *A* than for *B*. If assessment is accurate, but style is omitted from the data set, we are left with a positive relationship between AV and P^{31}.

Since the tax-saving variable, $m(AV' - AV)$, is constructed using AV, we find a problem. Assume the presence of a favorable omitted variable such as aluminum siding. *SP* and *AV* both appear large relative to their predicted values. Since *AV* must enter the tax-savings term with a negative sign, there is a negative relationship induced between tax savings and price. Note that the capitalization hypothesis predicts a positive relationship.

There are a number of ways by which proper assessment (AV') might be estimated. Initially it was decided to estimate Equation (5-15) in a first stage and then use the fitted values of AV to construct the tax-savings term. While this method was attractive because it did not require specific assumptions about assessors' targets, it made the problem of unobservables acute.

A closer examination of the two equations revealed that such a procedure was equivalent to including the negative of the residual for Equation (5-15) as a variable in Equation (5-21). That is:

$$\hat{AV} = \hat{a} + \Sigma \; \hat{b}_i X_i \qquad (5\text{-}23)$$

$$\hat{u} = AV - \hat{AV} \qquad (5\text{-}24)$$

The tax-savings term in Equation (5-21) is:

$$\lambda m(AV' - AV) \qquad (5\text{-}25)$$

Capitalization predicts that λ will have a positive sign. Significant omitted or unobservable information will lead to a very severe bias in the estimate of λ since omitted information implies a negative relationship between tax savings so constructed and selling price.

A slightly different construction illustrates the difficulty even more clearly. If we include the local tax rate as one of the *X*s, the same model can be rewritten in the following way:

$$AV' = \rho FmV \qquad (5\text{-}26)$$

$$FMV = \sum_i \beta_i X_i + e \qquad (5\text{-}27)$$

$$SP = FmV + \gamma m(\rho FmV - AV) + \xi \qquad (5\text{-}28)$$

where

FmV = Unobservable fair market value;
the value of the unit if it were properly
assessed.
SP = Selling price of the unit
AV = Actual assessed value of the unit
m = Local tax rate
AV' = Proper assessed value of the unit.

Substituting Equations (5-26) into (5-28) and (5-27) into (5-26) we obtain:

$$SP = \frac{AV'}{\rho} + \gamma m(AV' - AV) + \xi \qquad (5\text{-}29)$$

$$AV' = \rho \, \Sigma \, \beta_i X_i + e \qquad (5\text{-}30)$$

Reducing Equation (5-22) we obtain:

$$SP = \left(\frac{1}{\rho} + \gamma m \right) AV' - \gamma mAV + \xi \qquad (5\text{-}31)$$

and finally

$$SP = aAV' + bAV + \xi \qquad (5\text{-}32)$$

where

$$\gamma = \frac{-m}{b} \text{ and } \rho = \frac{1}{a - \gamma m}$$

Capitalization theory predicts a positive γ, which in turn predicts a negative b. To find such a relationship, AV' must capture the effects of *all* variables that affect both assessed and market value. It is unrealistic to expect any data set to yield a negative b.

Actually estimating Equations (5-30) and (5-31) by using Belmont data produced the following results:[f]

$$SP = \underset{(1610)}{1759} + \underset{(0.09)}{0.11AV'} + \underset{(0.09)}{1.15AV} \qquad (5\text{-}33)$$
$$ 1.09 \qquad\quad 1.21 \qquad\quad 12.9$$

$$\overline{R}^2 = 0.85 \quad N = 168$$

The powerful positive relationship between AV and SP even when the systematic variation in assessed value is controlled for provides strong evidence of a powerful omitted variable bias.

To demonstrate the effect of the bias, the California data and a subsample of the Boston data were used to estimate a series of regressions in which significant variables were sequentially dropped. At each step, one variable was dropped from both the first-stage assessed value equation and from the final run.

In each case, as explanatory information was excluded from the model, the absolute size and significance of the tax savings increased. In California, the coefficient on tax savings went from -53.5 ($t = 23.8$) to -62.5 ($t = 38.4$). Results are presented in Table 5-3.

Using Concord, Massachusetts, data, a similar exercise produced the same result. These estimations are presented in Table 5-4. In both cases, the coefficients of remaining endogenous variables change considerably as variation in the omitted variables was attributed to them. In general, researchers should be extremely cautious in their interpretations of hedonic price index coefficients unless data sets are extraordinarly complete.

To sum up the argument, empirical tests of the tax capitalization hypothesis are looking for a negative relationship between the random component of assessed value and selling price. The omission of any information that affects both selling price and assessed value will result in a biased estimate of the capitalization effect. If significant information is omitted, the random component of assessed value will be positively related to selling price and the capitalization effect may be unobservable.[g]

---

[f]Figures in parentheses are standard errors; figures in brackets are t-statistics.

[g]Additional evidence to this effect is gained from estimating Equations (5-14) and (5-15) using data from the five cities with the best data on structural

While two additional problems may potentially cause difficulties in estimating the capitalization of random assessment errors, neither is of particular concern here. The first is a problem of simultaneity; the second involves randomness in selling price.

It is possible that selling price and assessed value are related in a way not postulated in the simple capitalization models presented above. If, for example, assessors systematically underassess higher valued homes and overassess lower valued homes, there would appear to be a negative relationship between sales price and assessment rate. If such a relationship were to exist, using the characteristics to estimate the assessed value should identify the simultaneous system. In the Boston data it appears that assessment rates are remarkably consistent across value brackets. Assessment-sales ratios were calculated for each of thirteen price ranges for all towns in the sample. The results are presented in Table 5-5.

A second source of simultaneity might be a more direct relationship between sales price and assessed value. If buyers take an overassessment to indicate that the house is actually worth more, underassessed units would sell for more than the predicted sales price. There is no way to identify such an effect. Furthermore, the existence of such an effect would exacerbate the omitted variable bias documented above.

Finally, it was argued in Chapter 2 that market imperfections led to randomness in final selling price. If one were to use actual selling price to estimate the so-called proper tax bill, the results would be a significiantly biased estimate of the capitalization effect. For example, it might be suggested that a proper tax savings term might be

---

characteristics. Capitalization implies a positive λ; omitted variables result in consistently negative coefficients.

Estimates of Tax Savings Coefficient

Town	N	λ	t-Statistic	$\bar{R}^2$ Stage I	$\bar{R}^2$ Stage II
Concord	163	−20.3	−10.5	0.90	0.92
Melrose	171	−15.8	− 7.9	0.79	0.78
Weston	133	−12.7	− 4.9	0.70	0.75
Wellesley	315	−24.5	−18.8	0.82	0.90
Reading	230	−20.9	−18.1	0.75	0.88
Hanford, CA	1089	−52.6	−24.6	0.86	0.89

Table 5-3.   Omitted Variable Bias: California Data, N = 1084

	β_1	t_1	β_2	t_2	β_3	t_3	β_4	t_4	β_5	t_5	β_6	t_6
Constant	-24,970	11.3	-23,250	10.4	-18,630	8.4	-17,790	8.2	-15,370	7.1	-13,650	6.3
Lot Size	1,650	8.4	1,383	7.0	1,632	8.3	1,624	8.2	—	—	—	—
Floor Space	10.2	19.9	9.2	17.9	11.2	22.7	11.1	22.6	11.8	24.2	—	—
Rooms	-155	1.0	-191	1.2	-206	1.3	-186	1.2	-148	0.9	2,075	15.9
Quality	2,304	11.1	2,817	13.7	—	—	—	—	—	—	—	—
Year Built	116	12.5	—		—		—		—		—	
Baths	181	5.5	278	8.6	325	10.1	325	10.1	324	10.0	542	17.4
Fireplaces	2,073	8.4	2,036	8.1	2,598	10.5	2,601	10.5	2,679	10.8	4,739	20.1
Garage	18.7	0.5	26.1	0.8	91.2	2.6	95.5	2.8	99.5	2.9	541	1.6
Condition	241	4.4	368	6.8	530	10.0	541	10.2	582	11.2	850	16.4
Construction	-448	2.2	-391	1.9	356	1.8	—	—	—	—	—	—
Exterior Condition	-514	1.6	960	3.1	1,264	4.1	1,302	4.3	1,116	3.6	394	1.3
Heating	-58	0.7	-33	0.4	-193	2.3	-192	2.2	-300	3.5	-437	5.1
Basement (D)	1,470	1.7	-829	0.9	-627	0.7	-650	0.7	-681	0.7	4,276	5.0
Swim Pool (D)	4,142	9.3	3,877	8.6	4,041	8.9	4,009	8.9	4,055	8.9	5,896	13.1
Air Conditioning (D)	1,342	4.4	1,086	5.9	2,368	7.7	2,357	7.7	2,486	8.1	2,507	8.1
Sewer Tie-in (D)	1,704	1.8	2,190	2.3	1,962	2.1	1,924	2.1	1,431	2.0	-901	0.9
Neighborhood Quality (1-10)	448	5.8	304	3.9	529	6.9	549	7.3	600	7.9	928	12.4
Access	-21	3.2	9.4	6.3	14.4	2.3	14.3	2.3	13.7	2.1	-6.9	1.1
Tax Savings	-535	-23.8	-56.8	-21.1	-58.0	29.5	-57.9	29.4	-58.9	-30.3	-62.5	38.4
$\bar{R}^2$ Price Equation	.89		.89		.89		.89		.89		.89	
$\bar{R}^2$ Assessment Equation	.86		.85		.82		.82		.82		.73	

Table 5-4.   Omitted Variable Bias: Concord, Massachusetts, Data, $N = 163$

	β_1	t_1	β_2	t_2	β_3	t_3	β_4	t_4
Full Basement	-6,211	2.3	-6,010	2.3	-9,240	3.5	-1,022	3.9
Construction Quality	-3,451	7.4	-3,513	7.7	-4,429	10.1	-6,502	16.2
Rooms	40.5	0.1	70.5	0.2	208	0.6	2,707	9.1
Year Built	124	4.2	126	4.2	110	3.7	89.3	3.0
Modern Kitchen	1,032	0.8	1,080	0.8	2,681	2.2	1,564	1.3
Brick or Stone	-3,069	0.6	-3,041	0.7	-2,946	0.6	-4,027	0.9
One-Car Garage	068.3	0.0	111.5	0.1	374	0.3	-572	0.4
Two-Car Garage	1,671	1.3	1,695	1.3	3,320	2.5	5,089	3.8
Lot Size	.21	11.6	.21	11.6	.22	11.6	.22	11.8
Floor Space	4.00	3.3	4.20	3.6	9.7	11.5	—	—
Baths	988	6.9	981	6.8	—	—	—	—
Fireplaces	322	0.6	—	—	—	—	—	—
Tax Saving	-20.1	10.4	-19.2	10.2	-20.6	12.0	-21.8	16.6
$\bar{R}^2$ Price Equation	.92		.92		.92		.92	
$\bar{R}^2$ Assessment Equation	.90		.90		.88		.79	

$$TAXSAVE = m(AV - \widehat{AV})$$
$$\widehat{AV} = \Sigma \gamma_1 X_1$$

Table 5-5.   Assessment-Sales Ratios for Various Dwelling Unit Groupings

Unit Selling Price	Concord	Wellesley	Belmont	Saugus	Wakefield	Stoneham	Reading	Lincoln	Bedford	Arlington	Melrose	Weston	Waltham	Hanford
10–15,000	—	.45	—	1.03	.36	.52	—	—	—	—	.77	—	1.27	.97
15–20,000	.83	.35	—	.95	.29	.35	—	—	.57	1.06	1.00	—	.82	.91
20–25,000	.74	.72	.79	.79	.30	.31	.80	.84	.49	.84	.90	.56	.73	.96
25–30,000	.78	.73	.80	.82	.30	.32	.81	.56	.48	.81	.89	.56	.72	1.00
30–35,000	.75	.68	.80	.80	.30	.31	.82	.49	.45	.75	.89	.52	.77	.99
35–40,000	.76	.71	.78	.88	.33	.31	.83	.50	.45	.77	.86	.63	.77	.98
40–45,000	.78	.68	.76	—	.33	.35	.83	—	.47	.83	.82	.65	.81	1.01
45–50,000	.72	.67	.73	.78	.27	.28	.83	.64	.48	.81	.94	.56	.72	1.00
50–60,000	.78	.69	.78	—	—	—	.66	.64	.50	—	.93	.61	.94	.93
60–70,000	.84	.66	.71	—	—	—	.83	.55	.47	—	—	.64	—	.97
70–80,000	.80	.64	.77	—	—	—	—	.50	—	—	—	.58	—	1.09
80–90,000	.87	.64	.66	—	—	—	—	—	—	—	—	.58	—	—
>90	.81	.64	.70	—	—	—	—	.51	—	—	—	.59	—	—
Overall Mean	.78	.68	.76	.85	.30	.32	.82	.57	.47	.84	.90	.60	.77	1.01

$$\lambda m(\overline{AR} \cdot P - AV) \qquad\qquad (5\text{--}34)$$

where

m = Nominal tax rate
$\overline{AR}$ = Mean assessment rate for the town
P = Unit selling price
AV = Actual assessed value.

Inclusion of such a variable in a hedonic index with P as the dependent variable results in a positive and highly significant estimate of λ. Rather than evidence of tax capitalization, however, it is merely the result of including the random left-hand variable in a right-hand term. Again, using a prediction of AV based on the unit characteristics instead of $\overline{AR} \cdot P$ should wash out the random component in selling price.

✳ *Chapter 6*

Summary and Conclusions

The property tax is based on the so-called fair market value of unique heterogeneous assets that pass through the market only infrequently. As such the tax presents administrators and economists with a set of complex and interesting problems.

Since nominal property tax rates are generally uniform within jurisdictions, the way in which administrators value or assess properties determines the way in which the tax burden is divided up among community residents. The pattern of effective rates that emerges from the assessment process and the way in which assessments are changed through time determine the extent to which resource flows are distorted as well as the extent and direction of ultimate tax shifting.

This book is a theoretical discussion and an empirical exploration of property tax rate variation within jurisdictions. It is composed of four separable parts. The first part (Chapter 2) examines the extent of observed rate variation within various kinds of fiscal jurisdictions. The second part (Chapter 3) turns to economic theory to identify causes or potential causes of unintended rate variation. The third part (Chapter 4) uses three separate sets of data to empirically examine patterns of rate variation. The fourth part (Chapter 5) is a theoretical and empirical examination of one of the consequences of intrajurisdictional rate differences: tax capitalization.

The data presented in Chapter 2 reveal that assessment-sales ratios vary extensively within jurisdictions. Most studies, including this book, utilize a coefficient of dispersion around the town's mean (or median) assessment-sales ratio as an imperfect measure of performance. Census data based on 1971 sales show that one out of every ten properties sold was located in a jurisdiction where the so-called average property was 40 percent over- or underassessed. While suburban jurisdictions in the Boston Standard Metropolitan Statistical Area (SMSA) seem to do substantially better than the national average, the city of Boston itself does much worse. The amount of observed variation in assessment rates within Boston has grown dramatically in the past ten years. Performance varies more extensively from jurisdiction to jurisdiction among nonmetropolitan and smaller jurisdictions than it does among metropolitan and larger jurisdictions.

Very broadly speaking, variation in assessment rates within jurisdictions must come from one of two sources (1) randomness in selling price around its fair market value and (2) errors in estimating fair market value. Economic theory offers a variety of explanations for randomness in selling price. In housing markets, the most obvious source of random variation is imperfect information. In markets where both buyers and sellers search with uncertain information, market outcomes are equilibrium price distributions rather than equilibrium prices. This is compounded by the complex nature of housing and the resulting extent to which agents must rely upon available signals. The extent of variation in the selling price of a given housing unit should depend upon a variety of factors. Examples include (1) the presence or absence of informational intermediaries and their costs; (2) the rate of turnover and size of the market; and (3) the degree of informational exchange among sellers' agents (listing services or exclusive agent agreements), and so on.

Error in assessment may be either intentional or unintentional. The theoretical discussion in Chapter 3 focuses on unintentional errors likely to emerge from assessing techniques based on erroneous models of market price formation. The most frequently applied assessing methods are based on replacement costs. A substantial portion of any unit's value represents the capitalized value of economic rents as well as positive or negative quasi-rents associated with its less malleable characteristics. As a result these methods are likely to err in estimating the marginal values of locational characteristics and structural characteristics that are difficult to change.

Chapter 4 attempts to empirically sort out the causes of rate variation within jurisdictions. It is composed of three separate empirical studies: (1) a study of variation in the city of Boston, a city that has made no real attempt to assess properties with any precision; (2) an analysis of assessment bias using micro data from fourteen jurisdictions (3,284 observations) that do exert considerable efforts to distribute the tax burden in accordance with property values; and (3) a study of the determinants of variation utilizing macro or aggregate data on a substantial number of Massachusetts towns.

The most salient feature of Boston's assessing department is inertia. Properties more than thirty years old were assessed in 1946 and with few exceptions those assessments have not changed in the interim. While this is suggestive of simple inefficiency, there is no evidence to reject the hypotheses that this inertia represents a carefully calculated policy. Changes in individual neighborhoods are sufficient to explain changes in the pattern and level of assessment rates that took place during the 1960s. Such changes are sufficient to explain the mean level of assessment in 1960 assuming a 100 percent mean rate in 1946. However, rent and value changes are insufficient to explain the *pattern* of assessment rates across neighborhoods in 1960. There is significant evidence that original assessments were made at a lower than average rate on high-value properties and on owner-occupied units. There is also evidence that Roxbury was originally overassessed even when discounting for the small percentage of owner-occupied stock and for the low level of property values.

The second study in Chapter 4 uses detailed data on the structural and neighborhood characteristics of over 3,200 single family homes sold since 1971 to search for the sources of assessment error. It was estimated that approximately 21 percent of assessment error was systematic and could be explained. The majority of the explained error seems to emerge from the inaccurate valuation of neighborhood characteristics. A large portion of the remainder seems to result from erroneous valuation of the nonmalleable portions of the capital stock. These are precisely the sources of error that theory predicts given the nature of replacement cost assessing techniques.

The final portion of Chapter 4 examines patterns of variation in performance as measured by the coefficient of variation across a large number of Massachusetts towns. There were five significant conclusions: (1) larger jurisdictions, which are likely to have better integrated real estate markets and a larger volume of transactions, tend to have less variation in residential assessment rates than smaller communities; (2) assessment accuracy degenerates rapidly through time subsequent to major revaluation efforts; (3) the continuing level of administrative support exerted by assessing departments as measured by the level of expenditure does not seem to have a major effect on performance; (4) there seem to be significant economies of scale in assessing; and (5) the effects of environmental or community differences as proxied by population and rate of change in population are small relative to the effects of time lags in the assessment process.

Chapter 5 deals with tax capitalization. It begins with a discussion of the theory of tax capitalization and a review and critique of previous empirical studies. Using the micro data on individual houses sold since 1971, the empirical portion of Chapter 5 tests for capitalization of interjurisdictional rate variation and two types of intrajurisdictional rate variation: (1) variation that is systematic by neighborhood and (2) assessment differences not related to location, that is, random over- and underassessment. In addition to revealing evidence of capitalization across jurisdictions, the data are suggestive of capitalization of neighborhood-specific differentials within jurisdictions. Estimations that attempt to discern the capitalization of more random errors are plagued by serious biases that would preclude the identification of such effects even if they existed. Such biases have not been previously acknowledged in the literature and cast doubt on earlier studies that claim to capture the random capitalization effect.

From a policy perspective two conclusions stand out. First, traditional assessing techniques should be updated to consider more explicitly the valuation of locational characteristics and less malleable structural characteristics. Second, very significant gains in accuracy can be achieved through more frequent updating and revaluation even using the traditional methods. The use of an assessing system based in part on multiple regression estimates of hedonic price indexes offers assessors (1) an inexpensive and easy way to update existing assessments using data on current sales and (2) a technique that provides unbiased estimates of the values of locational characteristics and more malleable structural characteristics.

While a number of jurisdictions, including Cook County, Illinois, currently employ these techniques, the number is small[1]. As experience is gained, however, and more individuals are convinced not to fear useful statistical and computational techniques, this number will grow.

Notes

NOTES TO CHAPTER 1

1. U.S. Department of Commerce, Bureau of the Census, *Statistical Abstract of the United States* (Washington, D.C.: U.S. Government Printing Office, 1977), Table 460, p. 281.

2. The Constitution of the Commonwealth of Massachusetts as well as the General Laws establish that all property shall be assessed for tax purposes at "fair cash value." See Part II, Ch. 1, section 1, Article 4 of the Constitution of the Commonwealth of Massachusetts and General Laws (Ter. Ed.), Ch. 59, section 38.

3. The literature on interjurisdictional differentials has focused on capitalization; a substantial number of studies have empirically observed the capitalization phenomenon. Perhaps the most often cited paper is one of the earliest: Wallace Oates, "The Effects of Property Taxes and Local Public Spending on Property Values: An Empirical Study of Tax Capitalization and the Tiebout Hypothesis," *Journal of Political Economy*, 77 (November/December 1969): 957-971.

4. Henry Aaron, *Who Pays the Property Tax? A New View* (Washington, D.C.: Brookings Institution, 1975).

5. See Roger Brinner, "Inflation, Deferral and the Neutral Taxation of Capital Gains," *National Tax Journal* 26, 4 (December 1973): 565-573.

NOTES TO CHAPTER 2

1. U.S. Department of Commerce, Bureau of the Census, *Taxable Property Values and Assessment-Sales Price Ratios, 1972, Census of Governments*, vol. 2, part 2 (Washington, D.C.: U.S. Government Printing Office, 1972).

2. Ibid., p. 45, Table 3.

3. Frederick L. Bird, *The General Property Tax: Findings of the 1957 Census of Governments* (Washington, D.C.: U.S. Public Administration Service, 1960), p. 55.

4. Oliver Oldman and Henry Aaron, "Assessment-Sales Ratios under the Boston Property Tax," *National Tax Journal* (March 1965): 36-49.

5. Oldman and Aaron, op. cit., p. 48.

6. David E. Black, "Inequalities in Effective Property Tax Rates: A Statistical Study of the City of Boston," Ph.D. thesis, Massachusetts Institute of Technology, September 1969.

NOTES TO CHAPTER 3

1. Oldman and Aaron, Op. cit., p. 48.

2. Black, op. cit.

3. Ibid.

4. See G. Calabresi, "Transactions Costs, Resource Allocation, and Liability Rules—A Comment," *Journal of Law and Economics* 2 (1968):67-73.

5. George Stigler, "The Economics of Information," *Journal of Political Economy* 68 (June 1961):213-225.

6. See, for example, Michael Rothschild, "Models of Market Organization with Imperfect Information: A Survey" *Journal of Political Economy* 81 (December 1973):283-308.

7. Herman B. Leonard, "Theoretical Models of Search by Buyers and Sellers in Markets with Uncertain Information" (Thesis, Harvard University, 1974).

8. Ibid., p. 139.

9. See A. Michael Spence, *Market Signaling: Informational Transfer in Hiring and Related Screening Processes* (Cambridge, Mass.: Harvard University Press, 1974), especially Chapter 12, "Used Cars and the Absence of Effective Signaling."

10. For example, real estate agents, building and termite inspectors, and so on. For a brief discussion see Spence, op. cit., p. 112.

11. Edgar Olsen, "A Competitive Theory of the Housing Market," *American Economic Review* 59, 4 (September 1969):612.

12. A Mitchell Polinsky and Steven Shavell, "Amenities and Property Values in a General Equilibrium Model of an Urban Area," Working paper 1207-5 (Washington, D.C.: The Urban Institute, July 1973).

13. See, for example, John M. Quigley, "Residential Location: Multiple Work Places and a Heterogeneous Housing Stock," (Ph.D. dissertation, Harvard University, 1972); Gregory K. Ingram, "A Simulation Model of a Metropolitan Housing Market," (Ph.d. dissertation, Harvard University, 1971); Mahlon Straszheim, *An Econometric Analysis of the Urban Housing Market* (New York: National Bureau of Economic Research, 1974).

14. Rosen has demonstrated that even if all attributes are readily reproducible and where a sufficiently large number of units is available so that choice among

various combinations of $\{X\}$ and $\{N\}$ is continuous, the formation of equilibrium attribute prices is an extremely complex process. At any given consumer equilibrium there exists a rate at which that consumer is willing to substitute additional units of attribute i for other goods (or money). That is, for each consumer we can construct a set of bid functions for each attribute. Similarly, it is possible to define a set of offer functions for housing producers assuming current production of all attributes and a given technology. Rosen illustrates the process of equilibrium formation where goods possess only a single attribute. See Sherwin Rosen, "Hedonic Prices and Implicit Markets," *Journal of Political Economy* 82, 1 (January/February 1974):34.

15. Straszheim, op. cit, p. 26.

16. Ann Schnare and Raymond Struyk, "Segmentation in Urban Housing Markets" paper presented at the Committee on Urban Economics Conference on Housing Research, October 4-5, 1974, Washington University, St. Louis, Missouri.

17. Kain and Quigley found considerable variation in the structure of attribute prices between ghetto and nonghetto properties. See John Kain and John Quigley, *Housing Markets and Racial Discrimination* (New York: National Bureau of Economic Research, 1975).

A more recent test of segmentation was accomplished by the author as a part of a study of discrimination in nonmetropolitan housing utilizing data on about 1,000 housing transactions drawn from six states. The distribution of home values in rural areas is clearly bimodal. There is, in most areas, a stock of homes that are best described as shacks occupied only by the very poor. The difference of attribute prices between this portion of the housing market and other portions was substantial. See Janet Marantz, Karl Case, and Herman Leonard, *Discrimination in Rural Housing: Case Studies and Analysis of Six Selected Markets* (Lexington, Mass.: D.C. Heath, Lexington Books, 1976).

18. Makoto Ohta, "Production Technologies of the U.S. Boiler and Turbogenerator Industries and Hedonic Price Indexes for These Products," *Journal of Political Economy* 83,1 (February 1975).

19. U.S. Department of Commerce, Bureau of the Census, "Taxable Property Values and Assessment-Sales Price Ratios," *1972 Census of Government* vol. 2, part 1 (Washington, D.C.: U.S. Government Printing Office, 1973), Table A, p. 4.

20. See Robert Hall, "The Measurement of Quality Change from Vintage Price Data," and Phillip Cagen, "Quality Changes and the Purchasing Power of Money," both in *Price Indexes and Quality Change*, Zvi Griliches, ed. (Cambridge, Mass.: Harvard University Press, 1971), chs. 7 and 8.

21. See, for example, Gregory K. Ingram, John F. Kain, and J. Royce Ginn, *The Detroit Prototype of the N.B.E.R. Urban Simulation Model* (New York: National Bureau of Economic Research, 1972), pp. 109-123; Ira S. Lowry, "A Model of Metropolis," The Rand Corporation Memorandum RM-4035-RC (Santa Monica, Cal.: The Rand Corporation 1964); Frank de Leeuw, "The Distribution of Housing Services: A Mathematical Model," Working Paper 208-1, (Washington, D.C.: The Urban Institute, November 1971).

22. D.F. Bradford, R.A. Malt, and W.E. Oates, "The Rising Cost of Local Public Services: Some Evidence and Reflections," *National Tax Journal* 22 (June 1969), p. 201.

23. See, for example, Thomas C. Schelling, "A Process of Residential Segregation: Neighborhood Tipping," in *Racial Discrimination in Economic Life*, Anthony H. Pascal, ed. (Lexington, Mass.: D.C. Heath, Lexington Books, 1972); Karl E. and Alma Taeuber, *Negroes in Cities: Residential Segregation and Neighborhood Change* (Chicago: Aldine Publishing Co., 1965); David H. Karlen, *Racial Integration and Property Values in Chicago:* Urban Economics Report No. 7, April 1968 (Chicago: University of Chicago Press); and others.

24. See William Alonso, *Location and Land Use* (Cambridge, Mass.: Harvard University Press, 1964); Richard Muth, *Cities and Housing* (Chicago: University of Chicago Press, 1969); Edwin Mills, "An Aggregate Model of Resource Allocation in a Metropolitan Area," *American Economic Review* 57,2 (May 1967), pp. 197-211; John F. Kain, "The Journey to Work as a Determinant of Residential Location," *Papers and Proceedings of the Regional Science Association*, 9 (1962); and others.

25. See, especially, John F. Kain and John M. Quigley, *Discrimination and a Heterogeneous Housing Stock: An Economic Analysis* (New York: National Bureau of Economic Research, 1972), (processed); and Ann B. Schnare, *Externalities, Segregation and Housing Prices* (Washington, D.C.: The Urban Institute, 1974); Thomas King, *Property Taxes, Amenities, and Residential Land Values* (Cambridge, Mass.: Ballinger Publishing Co., 1973).

26. George E. Peterson, "The Effects of Zoning Regulations on Suburban Property Values," Working Paper 1204-24 (Washington, D.C.: The Urban Institute, March 1973).

27. F. Gerard, Grace Milgram, E.W. Green, and C. Mansfield, "Underdeveloped Land Prices During Urbanization: A Micro Empirical Study over Time," *Review of Economics and Statistics* 1, 2 (May 1968).

NOTES TO CHAPTER 4

1. See Oldman and Aaron, op. cit., and Chapter 2.

2. Oldman and Aaron computed assessment-sales ratios for individual unit types. This exercise was repeated for single family detached units only. Adjustment to 1946 levels was made using the increase in median value of owner-occupied units. The results were identical.

3. These two points are echoed in an early classic by Rudolf Goldscheid:

it depends upon social structure and upon the internal and external political constellations . . . whether the tax screw should be tightened or relieved, what groups of the population are to bear the heavier or the lighter burden . . . .

and tell me what you want to spend your money on, and I shall tell you by what means you will get the required revenue, what classes of society you must draw upon.

See Rudolf Goldscheid, "A Sociological Approach to Problems of Public Finance," reprinted in Richard Musgrave and Alan Peacock, eds., *Classics in the Theory of Public Finance* (New York: St. Martin's Press, 1967), pp. 202, 207.

4. See Brian J.L. Berry and Robert Bednarz, "A Hedonic Model of Prices and Assessments for Single Family Homes: Does the Assessor Follow the Market or the Market Follow the Assessor?" *Land Economics* 51, 1 (February 1975): 21-40.

5. Laura Berger et al., "The Feasibility of Applying Multiple Digression Analysis to the Assessment of Residential Properties in Massachusetts." Unpublished discussion paper, Department of City and Regional Planning, Harvard University, Cambridge, Mass., February 1976.

6. See D.F. Bradford, R.A. Malt, and W.E. Oates, "The Rising Cost of Local Public Services: Some Evidence and Reflections," *National Tax Journal* 22 (June 1969).

7. Universal Publishing Co., *Universal Atlas of Eastern Massachusetts*, (Boston, Mass., 1974) 9th ed.

8. See Berger et al., op. cit., Table 1, p. 9.

NOTES TO CHAPTER 5

1. See "The Property Tax: Progressive or Regressive?", series of papers presented at the 86th Annual Meeting of the American Economic Association, 1973, *American Economic Review*, 64, 2 (May 1974): 212-235.

2. Martis S. Feldstein, "On the Theory of Tax Reform." Discussion paper 408, Harvard Institute of Economic Research, Cambridge, Mass., April 1975.

3. See, for example, Peter Mieskowski, "The Property Tax: An Excise or Profits Tax," *Journal of Public Economics* 1 (April 1972): 73-96.

4. This analysis goes back at least to Ricardo and has been echoed by Pigou, Dalton, and more recently Mieskowski and Aaron. See D. Ricardo, *On the Principles of Political Economy and Taxation*, R. Sraffa, ed. (New York: Cambridge University Press, 1951); A.C. Pigou, *A Study in Public Finance*, 4th ed. (London: Routledge and Kegan Paul, 1954); Mieskowski, op. cit.; Henry Aaron, *Who Pays the Property Tax?* (Washington, D.C.: Brookings Institution, 1975).

5. Martin Feldstein, "The Surprising Incidence of a Tax on Pure Rent: A New Answer to an Old Question," *Journal of Political Economy* 85, 2 (April 1977): 349-360.

6. Arnold Harberger, "The Incidence of the Corporation Income Tax," *Journal of Political Economy* 70 (June 1962): 215-240.

7. While the supply side of housing markets has been receiving some attention in the literature of late, a great deal of work remains. One segment of the theoretical literature that has been virtually ignored by housing supply analysts, which has potentially a great deal to offer, examines the costs of adjustment from one optimal capital stock to another. See, for example, M.I.

Nadiri and S. Rosen, *A Disequilibrium Approach to the Demand for Factors of Production.*

8. M. Feldstein, "On the Theory of Tax Reform," op. cit.

9. Ibid., p. 36.

10. Jens P. Jensen, *Property Taxation in the United States* (Chicago: University of Chicago Press, 1931), pp. 64–75; and Darwin W. Daicoff, "Capitalization of the Property Tax," (Ph.D. dissertation, University of Michigan, 1961). Daicoff's results are reported in Dick Netzer, *Economics of the Property Tax* (Washington, D.C.: The Brookings Institution, 1966).

11. Larry Orr, "The Incidence of Differential Property Taxes on Urban Housing," *National Tax Journal* 21 (September 1968): 253–262; and Wallace Oates, "The Effects of Property Taxes and Local Public Spending on Property Values: An Empirical Study of Tax Capitalization and the Tiebout Hypothesis," *Journal of Political Economy* 77 (November-December 1969): 957–971.

12. Oates, op. cit., p. 968.

13. Edel and Sclar make an interesting and valid point about the interpretation of Oates's results as a confirmation of the Tiebout hypothesis. They claim his results only demonstrate that families have preferences about local public service levels and act accordingly. His results yield no evidence that there is an efficient market solution to the public goods dilemma. Since we are concerned with the tax side, this is of little import to the analysis below. See Matthew Edel and Elliott Sclar, "Taxes, Spending and Property Values: Supply Adjustment in a Tiebout Oates Model," *Journal of Political Economy* 82, 5 (September/October 1974): 941–954.

14. George Richard Meadows, "Taxes, Spending and Property Values: A Comment and Further Results," *Journal of Political Economy* 84, 4, part 1 (August 1976): 869–880.

15. A. Thomas King, "Estimating Property Tax Capitalization: A Criticial Comment," *Journal of Political Economy* 85, 2 (April 1977): 425–431.

16. Ibid., p. 427.

17. Ibid., p. 430.

18. Harvey Rosen and David J. Fullerton, "A Note on Local Tax Rates, Public Benefit Levels, and Property Values," *Journal of Political Economy* 85, 2 (April 1977): 433–440.

19. Ibid., p. 439.

20. Orr, op. cit.

21. Ibid., p. 261.

22. J.D. Heinberg and W.E. Oates, "The Increase of Differential Property Taxes on Urban Housing: A Comment and Some Further Evidence," *National Tax Journal* 23, 1 (March 1970): 92–98.

23. Ibid., p. 98. A similar critique by Black reestimates Orr's equations using a different set of variables and confirms his results. See David E. Black, "The Incidence of Differential Property Taxes on Urban Housing: Some Further Evidence," *National Tax Journal*, 26, 4 (Dec. 1973): pp. 565–573.

24. The two pioneering studies utilizing micro data do not address the issue. See John F. Kain and John Quigley, *Housing Markets and Racial Discrimina-*

tion (New York National Bureau of Economic Research, 1975); and Mahlon Straszheim, *An Econometric Analysis of the Urban Housing Market* (New York: National Bureau of Economic Research, 1975).

25. A. Thomas King, *Property Taxes, Amenities, and Residential Land Values* (Cambridge, Mass.: Ballinger Publishing Co., 1973).

26. Ibid., p. 54.

27. Ibid., p. 89.

28. It should also be noted that while King acknowledges the fact that a number of his variables are codetermined, he makes no allowance for that in his estimation procedure, which is ordinary least squares. At the very least, a two-stage procedure should have been utilized.

29. A.M. Church, "Capitalization on the Effective Property Tax Rate on Single Family Residences," *National Tax Journal* 27 (March 1974): 113–122.

30. King, "Estimating Property Tax Capitalization," op. cit.

31. Even Church's list of ninety characteristics leaves out a number of important items such as condition and age of a unit's roof, the type of siding, and so on. See Church, op. cit., p. 118.

NOTES TO CHAPTER 6

1. See, for example, Berger et al., op. cit., Berry and Bednarz, op. cit. and John Yinger, "Estimating the Market Value of Single Family Houses," a report on assessment procedures in the city of Madison, Wisconsin, June 1976.

Appendix

Table A-1. Area: Brighton

	1950	1960	1970	Δ1950–60	Δ1960–70
Total Population	59,057	62,778	63,657	+6.3	+1.4
Percent Black	0.1	0.4	1.8	—	—
Number of Families	20,213	16,029	14,667	-20.7	-8.5
Median Income	3,207	6,226	9,620	+94.1	+54.5
Percent $<$ Poverty[a]	22.2	9.9	6.4	—	—
Percent $<$ 1.5 · Poverty	37.9	23.4	13.5	—	—
Number of Housing Units	19,016	22,020	25,324	+15.8	+15.0
Percent Vacant[b]	1.3	2.6	2.1	—	—
Percent Lacking Some Plumbing[c]	3.1	3.3	1.2	—	—
Percent $>$ 1.01 Persons per Room	8.3	6.8	5.2	—	—
Median Value Owner Occupied	10,654	14,425	21,725	+35.4	+50.6
Median Contract Rent	46	79	135	+71.1	+70.1
Percent Owner Occupied			.18		

[a]1950: $2,000; 1960: $3,000.
[b]Total vacant (nonseasonal).
[c]No private bath, no running water, or dilapidated (1950-1960).
Note: *Tracts 1950-1960:* Y0001-Y0005—*Tracts 1970:* 0001-0008.

Table A-2. Area: Charlestown

	1950	1960	1970	Δ1950-60	Δ1960-70
Total Population	31,332	20,638	15,353	-34.1	-25.6
Percent Black	1.0	0.3	0.5	—	—
Number of Families	12,435	4,621	3,517	--62.8	-23.9
Median Income	2,473	5,242	8,606	+111.9	+64.2
Percent < Poverty[a]	44.3	21.5	13.8	—	—
Percent < 1.5 · Poverty	61.5	40.4	24.8	—	—
Number of Housing Units	6,957	6,443	5,119	-7.4	-20.5
Percent Vacant[b]	3.1	7.2	5.8	—	—
Percent Lacking Some Plumbing[c]	29.4	21.4	5.6	—	—
Percent > 1.01 Persons per Room	19.4	11.1	8.4	—	—
Median Value Owner Occupied	4,353	6,825	12,400	+56.8	+81.7
Median Contract Rent	27.5	42	73	+55.6	+73.8
Percent Owner Occupied			.30		

[a] 1950: $2,000; 1960: $3,000.

[b] Total vacant (nonseasonal).

[c] No private bath, no running water, or dilapidated (1950-1960).

Note: *Tracts 1950-1960:* C-0001-0003, D-0001-0004, E-0001-0002—*tracts 1970:* 0401- 0408.

Table A-3. Area: Dorchester

	1950	*1960*	*1970*	*Δ1950–1960*	*Δ1960–1970*
Total Population	186,476	173,422	176,891	-7.0	+2.0
Percent Black	0	0.6	27	—	—
Number of Families	55,643	43,402	39,756	-22.0	-8.4
Median Income	3,321	6,699	9,218	+101.7	+37.6
Percent < Poverty[a]	24.0	10.3	13.0	—	—
Percent < 1.5 · Poverty	42.0	23.6	23.5	—	—
Number of Housing Units	54,054	55,514	57,124	+2.7	+2.9
Percent Vacant[b]	1.0	2.9	6.8	—	—
Percent Lacking Some Plumbing[c]	5.1	3.1	2.1	—	—
Percent > 1.01 Persons per Room	7.9	6.7	8.3	—	—
Median Value Owner Occupied	9,779	12,800	15,459	+30.9	+20.8
Median Contract Rent	47	81	98	+71.1	+40.0
Percent Owner Occupied			.25		

[a]1950: $2,000; 1960: $3,000.
[b]Total vacant (nonseasonal).
[c]No private bath, no running water, or dilapidated (1950–1960).
Note: *Tracts 1950–1960:* T0001-0008, P0001-0006, Q0005, X0001—*tracts 1970:* 0901-0924, 1001-1011.

Table A-4.　Area: East Boston

	1950	1960	1970	Δ1950–1960	Δ1960–1970
Total Population	54,021	43,757	38,900	-19.0	-11.1
Percent Black	0	0.1	0.8	—	—
Number of Families	15,336	11,594	10,006	-24.4	-13.7
Median Income	2,706	5,043	8,450	+86.4	+67.6
Percent < Poverty[a]	28.6	20.0	10.3	—	—
Percent < 1.5 · Poverty	55.0	40.3	19.0	—	—
Number of Housing Units	14,610	14,069	13,718	-3.6	-2.5
Percent Vacant[b]	2.0	5.5	6.8	—	—
Percent Lacking Some Plumbing[c]	35.0	21.4	9.1	—	—
Percent > 1.01 Persons per Room	17.1	9.2	6.7	—	—
Median Value Owner Occupied	6,052	8,400	12,500	+38.8	+48.8
Median Contract Rent	25	42	66	+68.0	+57.1
Percent Owner Occupied			.28		

[a]1950: $2,000; 1960: $3,000.
[b]Total vacant (nonseasonal).
[c]No private bath, no running water, or dilapidated (1950-1960).
Note: *tracts 1950-1960:* A0001-0006, B0001-0005—*tracts 1970:* 501-512.

Table A-5. Area: Hyde Park

	1950	1960	1970	Δ1950–1960	Δ1960–1970
Total Population	39,277	37,077	38,264	-5.6	+3.2
Percent Black	0	0	1.0	—	—
Number of Families	11,674	9,479	9,527	-18.8	+0.5
Median Income	3,260	6,351	10,662	+94.8	+67.9
Percent < Poverty[a]	23.0	12.5	3.4	—	—
Percent < 1.5 · Poverty	41.6	24.6	11.5	—	—
Number of Housing Units	10,073	10,616	11,880	+5.4	+11.9
Percent Vacant[b]	1.0	2.4	2.0	—	—
Percent Lacking Some Plumbing[c]	17.5	6.1	2.3	—	—
Percent > 1.01 Persons per Room	11.0	6.8	5.8	—	—
Median Value Owner Occupied	9,339	13,000	19,100	+39.2	+46.9
Median Contract Rent	33	58	100	+75.8	+72.4
Percent Owner Occupied			.53		

[a] 1950: $2,000; 1960: $3,000
[b] Total vacant (nonseasonal).
[c] No private bath, no running water, or dilapidated (1950-1960).
Note: *tracts 1950-1960:* Z0001, A, B, C; Z0002—*tracts 1970:* 1401-1404.

Table A-6. Area: Roxbury

	1950	1960	1970	Δ1950-1960	Δ1960-1970
Total Population	101,791	66,164	62,856	-35.0	-5.0
Percent Black	13.	49.0	64.9	—	—
Number of Families	31,519	18,975	13,985	-39.8	-26.3
Median Income	2,510	4,675	6,443	+86.2	+37.8
Percent < Poverty[a]	30.0	28.0	24.0	—	—
Percent < 1.5 · Poverty	53.0	48.0	40.3	—	—
Number of Housing Units	29,355	28,005	23,356	-4.6	-16.6
Percent Vacant[b]	2.0	9.6	13.6	—	—
Percent Lacking Some Plumbing[c]	27.3	15.2	2.7	—	—
Percent > 1.01 Persons per Room	16.0	11.3	10.1	—	—
Median Value Owner Occupied	5,768	8,083	10,933	+40.1	+35.2
Median Contract Rent	33	49	85	+48.5	+73.5
Percent Owner Occupied			.13		

[a]1950: $2,000; 1960: $3,000.
[b]Total vacant (nonseasonal).
[c]No private bath, no running water, or dilapidated (1950–1960).
Note: *tracts 1950–1960:* Q-0001–0004, R-0001–0003, S-0002–0006, V-0001–0002, U-000 -0006—*tracts 1970:* 0801–0821.

Table A-7. Area: South Boston

	1950	1960	1970	Δ1950–1960	Δ1960–1970
Total Population	51,312	43,051	38,488	−16.1	−10.6
Percent Black	0	0	1.0	—	—
Number of Families	16,127	10,563	9,148	−34.5	−13.4
Median Income	2,530	4,891	8,707	+93.3	+78.8
Percent < Poverty[a]	26.6	15.3	9.9	—	—
Percent < 1.5 · Poverty	47.5	31.6	20.0	—	—
Number of Housing Units	14,423	14,639	14,259	+1.5	−2.6
Percent Vacant[b]	1.3	4.8	4.7	—	—
Percent Lacking Some Plumbing[c]	20.7	12.0	4.8	—	—
Percent > 1.01 Persons per Room	17.0	9.5	7.0	—	—
Median Value Owner Occupied	4,828	7,801	11,500	+61.6	+47.4
Median Contract Rent	31.3	48	78	+53.4	+62.6
Percent Owner Occupied			.24		

[a]1950: $2,000; 1960: $3,000.
[b]Total vacant (nonseasonal).
[c]No private bath, no running water, or dilapidated (1950–1960).
Note: *tracts 1950–1960:* M-0001–0004, N0001–0004, 0-0001–0004, P-0001, A, B, T-0001—
tracts 1970: 0601—0614.

Table A-8.   Area: West Roxbury

	1950	1960	1970	Δ1950–1960	Δ1960–1970
Total Population	28,427	30,019	31,190	+5.6	+3.9
Percent Black	0	0	2.0	—	—
Number of Families	8,037	7,811	7,843	-2.8	+0.4
Median Income	4,377	7,991	13,005	+82.6	+62.7
Percent < Poverty[a]	14.0	5.8	3.3	—	—
Percent < 1.5 · Poverty	25.1	13.1	5.9	—	—
Number of Housing Units	8,180	9,161	9,821	+12.0	+7.2
Percent Vacant[b]	1.7	1.2	1.1	—	—
Percent Lacking Some Plumbing[c]	1.1	1.0	1.2	—	—
Percent > 1.01 Persons per Room	3.7	2.9	3.5	—	—
Median Value Owner Occupied	12,369	16,900	23,900	+36.6	+41.4
Median Contract Rent	60	94	136	+56.7	+44.7
Percent Owner Occupied			.65		

[a]1950: $2,000; 1960: $3,000.
[b]Total vacant (nonseasonal).
[c]No private bath, no running water, or dilapidated (1950–1960).
Note: *tracts 1950–1960:* W0006, A, B, C, D—*tracts 1970:* 1301–1304.

Bibliography

Aaron, Henry. "A New View of Property Tax Incidence." *American Economic Review* 64,2 (May 1974):212-221.

—— *Who Pays the Property Tax? A New View.* Washington, D.C.: Brookings Institution, 1975.

Alonso, William. *Location and Land Use.* Cambridge, Mass.: Harvard University Press, 1964.

Auto Data Systems. *Real Estate Transfer Directory.* Framingham, Mass., 1971 and 1973.

Berger, Laura; Bruckenstein, Barbara; Craig, Barbara; Davis, E. Winn; Grist, Howard; Ladd, Gridley; Perry, Stephen; and Schoonmaker, Kathleen. "The Feasibility of Applying Multiple Regression to the Assessment of Residential Property in Massachusetts." Unpublished discussion paper, Department of City and Regional Planning, Harvard University, Cambridge, Mass., February 1976.

Berry, Brian, and Bednarz, Robert. "A Hedonic Model of Prices and Assessments for Single Family Homes: Does the Assessor Follow the Market or the Market Follow the Assessor." *Land Economics*, 51, 1 (February 1975):21-40.

Bird, Frederick L. *The General Property Tax: Findings of the 1957 Census of Governments.* Washington, D.C., U.S. Public Administration Service, 1960.

Black, David E. "The Incidence of Differential Property Taxes on Urban Housing: Some Further Evidence." *National Tax Journal* 22, 2 (June 1974): 367-369.

—— "Inequalities in Effective Property Tax Rates: A Statistical Study of the City of Boston." Ph.D. thesis, Massachusetts Institute of Technology, September 1969.

Bradford, D.F.; Malt, R.A.; and Oates, W.E. "The Rising Cost of Local Public Services: Some Evidence and Reflections." *National Tax Journal* 22 (June 1969).

Brinner, Roger. "Inflation, Deferral and the Neutral Taxation of Capital Gains." *National Tax Journal* 26, 4 (December 1973):565-573.

Cagen, Phillip. "Quality Changes and the Purchasing Power of Money," in Zvi Griliches, ed. *Price Indexes and Quality Change.* Cambridge, Mass.: Harvard University Press, 1971.

Calabresi, Guido. "Transactions Costs, Resource Allocation, and Liability Rules—A Comment." *Journal of Law and Economics* 2 (1968):67-73.

Church, A.M. "Capitalization of the Effective Property Tax Rate on Single Family Residences." *National Tax Journal* 27 (March 1974):113-122.

Commonwealth of Massachusetts, Department of Corporations and Taxation. *1976 Equalized Valuations of Massachusetts Cities and Towns: Selected Tax Base Information.* Boston, Mass., April 1977.

Daicoff, Darwin W. "Capitalization of the Property Tax" Ph.D. dissertation, University of Michigan, 1961.

deLeeuw, Frank. "The Distribution of Housing Services: A Mathematical Model." Washington, D.C.: The Urban Institute, Working Paper 208-1, November 1971.

Edel, Matthew, and Sclar, Elliott. "Taxes, Spending and Property Values: Supply Adjustment in a Tiebout-Oates Model." *Journal of Political Economy* 82, 5 (September/October 1974):941-954.

Feldstein, Martin. "On the Theory of Tax Reform." Harvard Institute of Economic Research, Discussion Paper No. 408, Cambridge, Mass., April 1975.

—— "The Surprising Incidence of a Tax on Pure Rent: A New Answer to an Old Question." *Journal of Political Economy* 85, 2 (April 1977):349-360.

Gerard, F.; Milgram, Grace; Green, E.W.; and Mansfield, C. "Underdeveloped Land Prices During Urbanization: A Micro Empirical Study over Time." *Review of Economics and Statistics* 1, 2 (May 1968).

Goldscheid, Rudolf. "A Sociological Approach to Problems of Public Finance." Reprinted in Musgrave, Richard, and Peacock, Alan, eds. *Classics in the Theory of Public Finance.* New York: Macmillan, St. Martins Press, 1967.

Hall, Robert. "The Measurement of Quality from Vintage Price Data," in Zvi Grilliches, (ed.) *Price Indexes and Quality Change.* Cambridge, Mass.: Harvard University Press, 1971.

Harberger, Arnold. "The Incidence of the Corporation Income Tax." *Journal of Political Economy* 70 (June 1972):215-240.

Heinberg, J.D., and Oates, Wallace. "The Incidence of Differential Property Taxes on Urban Housing: A Comment and Some Further Evidence." *National Tax Journal* 23, 1 (March 1970):92-98.

Ingram, Gregory K. "A Simulation Model of a Metropolitan Housing Market." Ph.D. thesis, Harvard University, 1971.

Ingram, Gregory K.; Kain, John F.; and Ginn, J. Royce. *The Detroit Prototype of the N.B.E.R. Urban Simulation Model.* New York: National Bureau of Economic Research, 1972.

Jensen, Jens P. *Property Taxation in the United States.* Chicago: University of Chicago Press, 1931.

Kain, John F. "The Journey to Work as a Determinant of Residential Location." *Papers and Proceedings of the Regional Science Association*, vol. 9, 1962.

Kain, John F., and Quigley, John M. *Housing Markets and Racial Discrimination.* New York: National Bureau of Economic Research, 1975.

Karlen, David. *Racial Integration and Property Values in Chicago.* Urban Economics Report No. 7. Chicago: University of Chicago Press, April 1968.

King, A. Thomas. "Estimating Property Tax Capitalization: A Critical Comment." *Journal of Political Economy* 85, 2 (April 1977):425-431.

King, Thomas. *Property Taxes, Amenities and Residential Land Values.* Cambridge, Mass.: Ballinger Publishing Co., 1973.

Leonard, Herman. "Theoretical Models of Search by Buyers and Sellers in Markets with Uncertain Information." Honors thesis, Harvard University, 1974.

Lowry, Ira S. "A Model of Metropolis." The RAND Corporation Memorandum RM-4035-RC, Santa Monica, 1964.

Marantz, Janet; Case, Karl E.; and Leonard, Herman. *Discrimination in Rural Housing: Case Studies and Analysis of Six Selected Markets.* Lexington, Mass.: D.C. Heath, Lexington Books, 1976.

Meadows, George R. "Taxes, Spending and Property Values: A Comment and Further Results." *Journal of Political Economy* 84, 4, 1 (August 1976):869-880.

Mieskowski, Peter. "The Property Tax: An Excise or Profits Tax." *Journal of Public Economics* 1 (April 1972):73-96.

Mills, Edwin. "An Aggregate Model of Resource Allocation in a Metropolitan Area." *American Economic Review* (May 1967):197-211.

Musgrave, Richard. "Is the Property Tax on Housing Regressive?" *American Economic Review* 64, 2 (May 1974):222-229.

Musgrave, Richard A., and Peggy B. *Public Finance in Theory and Practice.* New York: McGraw-Hill, 1973.

Nadiri, M.I., and Rosen, Sherwin. *A Disequilibrium Approach to the Demand for Factors of Production.* New York: National Bureau of Economic Research, 1973.

Netzer, Dick. *Economics of the Property Tax.* Washington, D.C.:Brookings Institution, 1966.

Oates, Wallace. "The Effects of Property Taxes and Local Public Spending on Property Values: An Empirical Study of Tax Capitalization and the Tiebout Hypothesis." *Journal of Political Economy*, 77 (November/December 1969): 957-971.

Ohta, Makoto. "Production Technologies of the U.S. Boiler and Turbogenerator Industries and Hedonic Price Indexes for These Products." *Journal of Political Economy* 83, 1 (February 1975):1-25.

Oldman, Oliver, and Aaron, Henry. "Assessment-Sales Ratios Under the Boston Property Tax." *National Tax Journal* 18 (March 1965):36-49.

Olsen, Edgar. "A Competitive Theory of the Housing Market." *American Economic Review*, 59, 4 (September 1969):612-645.

Orr, Larry. "The Incidence of Differential Property Taxes on Urban Housing." *National Tax Journal* 21 (September 1968):253-262.

Peterson, George E. "The Effects of Zoning Regulations on Suburban Property Values." Working Paper #1204-4, The Urban Institute, March 1973.

Pigov, A.C. *A Study in Public Finance*, 4th ed. London: Routledge and Kegan Paul, 1954.

Polinsky, A. Mitchell, and Shavell, Steven. "Amenities and Property Values in a Model of an Urban Area." *Journal of Public Economics* 5 (1976):119-129.

Quigley, John M. "Residential Location: Multiple Work Places and a Heterogeneous Housing Stock." Ph.D. thesis, Harvard University, 1972.

Ricardo, David. *On the Principles of Taxation and Political Economy*, ed., P. Sraffa. New York: Cambridge University Press, 1951.

Rosen, Harvey, and Fullerton, David J. "A Note on Local Tax Rates, Public Benefit Levels, and Property Values." Journal of Political Economy 85, 2 (April 1977):433-440.

Rosen, Sherwin. "Hedonic Prices and Implicit Markets." Journal of Political Economy 82, 1 (January/February 1974):34.

Rothschild, Michael. "Models of Market Organization with Imperfect Information: A Survey." *Journal of Political Economy* 81 (December 1973):283-308.

—— "On the Cost of Adjustment." *Quarterly Journal of Economics* 85, 4 (November 1971):605-622.

Schnare, Ann B. *Externalities, Segregation and Housing Prices.* Washington, D.C.: Urban Institute, 1974.

Schnare, Ann, and Struyk, Raymond. "Segmentation in Urban Housing Markets." Paper presented at the Committee on Urban Economics' Conference on Housing Research, Washington University, St. Louis, Missouri, October 4-5, 1974.

Schelling, Thomas. "A Process of Residential Segregation: Neighborhood Tipping," in Anthony Pascal, ed. *Racial Discrimination in Economic Life.* Lexington, Mass.: D.C. Heath, Lexington Books, 1972.

Spence, A. Michael. *Market Signaling: Informational Transfer in Hiring and Related Screening Processes.* Cambridge, Mass.: Harvard University Press, 1974.

Stigler, George. "The Economics of Information." *Journal of Political Economy* 68 (June 1961):213-25.

Straszheim, Mahlon. *An Econometric Analysis of the Urban Market.* New York: National Bureau of Economic Research, 1974.

Taeuber, Karl E., and Taeuber, Alma F. *Negroes in Cities: Residential Segregation and Neighborhood Change.* Chicago: Aldine Publishing Co., 1965.

Tax Foundation. *Facts and Figures on Government Finance, 1975.* New York: Tax Foundation, Inc., 1975.

U.S. Department of Commerce, Bureau of the Census. *1970 Census of Population and Housing, Census Tracts, Boston, Massachusetts.* Washington, D.C.: U.S. Government Printing Office, 1971.

—— *Taxable Property Values and Assessment-Sales Ratios, 1972 Census of Governments*, vol. 2, part 2. Washington, D.C.: U.S. Government Printing Office, 1973.

Universal Atlas of Eastern Massachusetts, 9th ed. Boston: Universal Publishing Co., 1974.

Yinger, John. "Estimating the Market Value of Single Family Houses," A Report to the City of Madison, Wisconsin, June 1976.

Index

About the Author

Karl E. Case is an economist. His research has been in the areas of taxation and housing. He is currently working on projects for the Department of Housing and Urban Development studying the Urban Homesteading Program and the operations of the Urban Reinvestment Task Force. His previous publications include *Discrimination in Rural Housing* (D.C. Heath, Lexington Books, Lexington, Mass.) with Herman Leonard and Janet Marantz. He holds the Ph.D. in economics from Harvard University and has been on the faculties of Harvard and Harvard Law School. He is currently Assistant Professor of Economics at Wellesley College.